Yuriy Lukanov

The Press

How Russia destroyed Media Freedom in Crimea

With a foreword by Taras Kuzio

UKRAINIAN VOICES

Collected by Andreas Umland

The book series "Ukrainian Voices" publishes English- and German-language monographs, edited volumes, document collections, and anthologies of articles authored and composed by Ukrainian politicians, intellectuals, activists, officials, researchers, and diplomats. The series' aim is to introduce Western and other audiences to Ukrainian explorations, deliberations and interpretations of historic and current, domestic, and international affairs. The purpose of these books is to make non-Ukrainian readers familiar with how some prominent Ukrainians approach, view and assess their country's development and position in the world. The series was founded, and the volumes are collected by Andreas Umland, Dr. phil. (FU Berlin), Ph. D. (Cambridge), Associate Professor of Politics at the Kyiv-Mohyla Academy and an Analyst in the Stockholm Centre for Eastern European Studies at the Swedish Institute of International Affairs.

Yuriy Lukanov

THE PRESS

How Russia destroyed Media Freedom in Crimea

With a foreword by Taras Kuzio

ibidem
Verlag

Bibliographic information published by the Deutsche Nationalbibliothek

Die Deutsche Nationalbibliothek lists this publication in the Deutsche Nationalbibliografie; detailed bibliographic data are available in the Internet at http://dnb.d-nb.de.

Bibliografische Information der Deutschen Nationalbibliothek

Die Deutsche Nationalbibliothek verzeichnet diese Publikation in der Deutschen Nationalbibliografie; detaillierte bibliografische Daten sind im Internet über http://dnb.d-nb.de abrufbar.

ISBN-13: 978-3-8382-1784-0

© *ibidem*-Verlag, Stuttgart 2023

Printed in the United States of America

Content

Preface

Russia's Soviet-Style Repression of Media and Freedom of Speech in Occupied Crimea

The first edition of the book you are holding now is evidence of alleged criminal activity by the „courts" of the Russian-occupied Crimean city of Feodosia. This is not an exaggeration. In Russia, books have been cited as proof of crimes, as they were in the Soviet Union.

Iryna Danylovych is a nurse, as well as a citizen journalist. Nowadays, it is not unusual to have such a combination of commitments in Russian-occupied Crimea, where Danylovych is currently serving a seven-year sentence on fraudulent charges After Russia's illegal annexation of Crimea in February 2014, Russian authorities created unbearable conditions for professional journalists to work, leading to the phenomenon of citizen journalism. People from various professions began to disseminate information about what was truly taking place in Russian-occupied Crimea.

Danylovych published a blog, which was devoted to questions of medicine, but which also highlighted the political repression of all those who disagreed with Russia's occupation. Goons from the FSB (Federal Security Service), Russia's domestic successor to the Soviet Union's KGB, kidnapped her by forcing her into a car, and illegally imprisoned her in a basement for nine days without any criminal charges or the provision of legal assistance. She was threatened, subjected to extreme psychological pressure, and her eyes were exposed to a noxious mixture. The FSB's so-called „investigation" accused her of manufacturing explosives, and claimed she was a terrorist. Danylovych faces up to eight years' imprisonment and a fine of up to 100,000 Russian rubles. Her experience is not uncommon. Her story is found with many other trumped-up cases throughout Crimea.

Yuriy Lukanov has updated the second edition of his book with new documentary information dedicated to the phenomenon of such brave citizen journalism in Crimea.

Russia's annexation of Crimea in spring 2014 was not only a blatant act of military aggression and violation of international law, it went far deeper. Lukanov's detailed book-length study is the first collated publication of memoirs and the evidence of journalists about the Russian authorities' repression of the media in Crimea since 2014. Media freedom has become far worse since Russia has become more like a fascist, totalitarian dictatorship after the constitution was changed in 2020 to allow Vladimir Putin to be de facto president for life.

Lukanov's book covers in depth the abuse of human rights and freedom of speech in Crimea under the Russian occupation, with detailed case studies of the repression of and extreme violence against journalists. Russia's annexation of Crimea led to the return of Soviet-era repression of Crimean Tatars, Ukrainians and Russians: indeed, anybody opposed to Russia's illegal occupation.

Heavy-handed repression of the media has gone hand-in-hand with discrimination against Crimean Tatars and what the author calls 'Ukrainophobic chauvinism'. Occupied Crimea has been flooded by FSB officers who eavesdrop, place under surveillance, undertake the wanton destruction of property, perpetrate savage acts of violence, detain under false accusations, and hold mock trials and convict journalists and civic activists.

President Vladimir Putin's occupation regime is undertaking systematic repression in Crimea of the kind last seen in the dark days of the Soviet Union. This includes the closing down and corporate raiding of media outlets, and the use of vigilante thugs (*titushky*) to severely beat journalists and, in some cases, murder civil-society activists. Peaceful pickets and protests are violently broken up and their participants savagely beaten, arrested, and convicted on spurious Soviet-style charges.

This book covers those areas that relate to the suppression of media freedom in Russian-occupied Crimea. These include the expulsion of the Organization for Security and Cooperation in Europe (OSCE) from Crimea because the Kremlin does not want them collecting information and reporting the destruction of media freedom.

Lukanov's book also analyses how the Russian occupation authorities have undertaken steps to establish a Putin-friendly monopoly over the media in Crimea. Lukanov analyses how the FSB, the Ministry of Interior, the Prosecutor's office, and Cossacks and Russian extremist nationalist vigilantes have undertaken corporate raids on Ukrainian and Tatar media outlets. They have also used physical violence against journalists and civic activists, put on trial members of their families and thrown out of work journalists who refuse to toe the line on Russia's occupation of Crimea.

This book sheds light on a new wave of political repression of Crimean Tatars that began after Russia's occupation. Half of the Crimean Tatar people died during the Soviet authorities' ethnic cleansing of them from Crimea to Central Asia in 1944 on false charges of „collaboration with the Nazis". Crimean Tatars are banned from commemorating their genocide in 1944 in May of each year. They were only allowed to begin returning to Crimea in the late 1980s and 1990s, and by 2014 accounted for 15 percent of the Crimean population. Since 2014, under Russian occupation, Crimean Tatar leaders have been expelled and imprisoned, their media outlets have been closed, and the unofficial parliament, *Mejlis*, has been banned.

Lukanov's detailed study of the infringement of human rights and media freedom in Russian-occupied Crimea is important documentary evidence for journalists, academics, civic activists, and policymakers. This extensive and groundbreaking study should be widely circulated to Western governments, media, and experts. The world needs to know about Putin's use of Soviet-style political repression in a territory that he has illegally annexed.

Taras Kuzio is a professor of political science at the National University of Kyiv Mohyla Academy. In November 2010, he published *The Crimea: Europe's Next Flashpoint?* which forecast Russia's invasion and occupation four years later. His 2022 book *Russian Nationalism and the Russian-Ukrainian War* won the 2022 Petersen Literary Fund prize. His newest book is *Genocide and Fascism. Russia's War Against Ukrainians*.

Taras Kuzio

Introduction

On February 27, 2014 at four o'clock in the morning, armed men in unmarked uniform captured the premises of the Council of Ministers and the Verkhovna Rada of the Autonomous Republic of Crimea. With bitter irony, the journalists compared it with the attack of Nazi Germany on the Soviet Union. Then, on June 22, 1941, the war started at four o'clock in the morning, too.

Just over a week before, on February 18-20, at the Independence Square in Kyiv, more than eighty people were shot. The funeral ceremony was held in the same place, at Independence Square, accompanied by a sad melody of the song "Duck's floating."

After this terrible crime, the pro-Russian President of Ukraine, Viktor Yanukovych fled to Russia. His government fled together with him. The country was dominated by anarchy. The opposition supporting the Maidan, which came to power after its victory, did not have time to form a Cabinet of Ministers. This is when the government buildings in Simferopol were occupied.

Hot discussions during the pro-Russian rally in Simferopol.
Photo by Yuriy Lukanov

The next day after the capture, Simferopol was raging. People were walking down the streets with the Russian tricolor and shouting slogans urging Russia to come to the peninsula. The streets were are also full of organized groups of young men in sportswear or militarized uniform with St. George's ribbons on their chests. These ribbons were the symbols of the Russian Empire.

They called themselves the "self-defense of Crimea." They held campaigns near Ukrainian military units and then started blocking and capturing them together with the Russian military men.

As the subsequent events showed, most of the activists and organizers of these rallies were imported from Russia. In fact, these riots were organized by Putin's Russia, which has been developing the policy of annexing foreign territories for years.

The pro-Ukrainian citizens, who came out with the slogan "*Crimea is Ukraine*", opposed them. The Crimean Tatars, the indigenous people of Crimea, who yet in the 40s' of the last century experienced the imperial colonization policy of Moscow, being deported by the Stalin's regime and being able to return home after the USSR collapse only, were particularly active.

No one doubted that the seizure was made by members of the Russian armed forces. It was clear that Russia started the campaign of the occupation of Crimea, an act further continued by the war in Donbas and cost thousands of lives and millions of broken destinies.

Russia has ignored the Budapest Memorandum, which it signed with the US and the UK, ensuring the territorial integrity of Ukraine in exchange for Ukraine's giving up of the nuclear weapons located on its territory. One of the guarantors of Ukraine's territorial integrity hypocritically violated this integrity after 20 years.

On February 27, the Verkhovna Rada of Crimea, at an extraordinary session in the presence of the armed Russian military men, scheduled a "referendum" on the state independence of Crimea for May 25. This resolution was contrary to the Constitution of Ukraine and international law established after World War II. Then the date of the illegal "referendum" was adjourned twice. Finally, it was held hastily on March 16. Numerous witnesses say that the results of the "referendum" were rigged.

Rally for Ukraine in Simferopol. Photo by Yuriy Lukanov.

The residents of Simferopol, as well as the entire peninsula, told to each other the rumors that "fierce nationalists" from western Ukraine are going to come to Crimea, carry out a genocide of the Russian-speaking Crimeans and instill their "Nazi" order. All this allegedly was done with the consent of Kyiv, where the "fascist junta" seized power.

The pressure was maintained through the Russian media popular in the peninsula, which rapidly spread the fake news. Besides this, they were played up by many local media, on which the Russians had decisive influence.

> The author of these lines had a very revealing dialogue on a bus. I asked where I'd better get out.
> - Are you a visitant? — an elderly woman asked me instead of answering.
> - Yes.
> Are you not from Western Ukraine? — according to the disseminated mythology, the greatest Crimea haters live in Western Ukraine.
> - No, I'm from Kyiv.
> - Did you come to us with good intentions?

A major role in this shameful campaign was played by the Kremlin-controlled Russian media, which have been working for several years, deliberately washing the brains of not only the residents of the peninsula, but also of all Ukrainians.

"Crimean audience listened to the Russian news about events on the Maidan," describes the current situation, the author of the Annexation of Crimea, **Myroslav Mamchak**, a military journalist. *"Russian media described Maidan as Nazis' riot against the legitimate authority. The government, which replaced Yanukovych, was called "fascist junta" by the Russian media. This coined term was repeated by Crimean media, followed by the inhabitants of the peninsula.*

Scared Crimean officials not only repeated, but also invented dramatic situations on their own. This is how the rumors about Nazi troops appeared, which nobody has ever seen in Crimea, but everybody knows that they are ready to come to Crimea and arrange the massacre of civilians. They were discussed and feared, especially among the older generation. The 'witnesses' of their crimes began to appear.

The inflation of the 'anti-fascist' hysteria and dread in the face of the imaginary "Maidan Nazis" appeared to be quite efficient. The people were psychologically determined to seek salvation. Where? Certainly, asking the 'great and brotherly Russia' to protect them from the "bloody maniacs" of Kyiv. This is how the Russian propaganda worked."

Participants of the pro-Ukrainian rally near the military base in Simferopol are singing the Ukrainian national anthem. Photo by Yuriy Lukanov.

Later the Russian Vesti newspaper reported that Russian President Vladimir Putin, by a secret decree No. 269 awarded 300 Russian journalists for *"high professionalism and objectivity in covering the events in the Republic of Crimea."*

"Professionalism" and "objectivity" implied that many Russian journalists repeated Putin's lie that there were no Russian military men in the peninsula, that the government buildings were captured not by military fighters, but by so-called "self-defense" brigades of Crimea. Putin himself rejected these allegations after the annexation. Now he repeats the same thing about the Donbas, where Moscow has launched a war.

Those journalists in Crimea, who honestly spoke about the usurpation of the region, immediately encountered resistance and aggression on the part of the Russia-appointed occupation authorities, pro-Russian activists and Russian military men. During the illegal annexation and after the so-called "referendum", when Russia established its power in the peninsula, they resorted to various measures to block the spread of true information about their criminal acts. These measures were not spontaneous and casual; there worked and continues to work a whole machine to suppress freedom of speech. It has almost squeezed free journalism out of Crimea.

However, Crimean journalists, who remained faithful to their professional duty and Ukraine, continue to work despite all these difficulties. Their daily work does not allow forgetting or getting round the "Crimean problem", which has created a precedent of the most flagrant violation of international order established after World War II. They remind us every day that Crimea is part of Ukraine.

This book primarily consists of evidence from Crimean journalists about how Russia struggled with them. Most of them continue to believe that the state crime committed by the Russian Federation will not remain unpunished, and that Crimea will return to Ukraine.

Mayhem Panorama

OSCE, the UN and Obama Being Expelled from Crimea

On March 5, 2014, a crowd of several dozen people gathered in front of the Ukraina hotel in Simferopol. People gathered because the OSCE representative for freedom of speech, **Dunja Mijatovic**, was there.

It was a "cocktail" of older people and representatives of the so-called "Crimean self-defense." In the foreground, mainly female pensioners stood, with homemade placards in their hands, containing appeals in English to President Obama and the West generally not to interfere in the internal affairs of Ukraine and Crimea. The slogans contained numerous grammatical errors.

A crowd protests against the visit of the OSCE representative for media freedom Dunja Mijatovic to Crimea. Photo by Yuriy Lukanov.

The crowd chanted „*Russia! Russia!*" One of the event participants, a woman of retirement age, who did not give her name, told the author of these lines, *"We do not need the intervention of the West. Let America sort out its own affairs."*

Another woman of retirement age, having learned that a journalist was working at the local TV channel Chornomorka, which was banned by the occupiers from broadcasting, repeatedly called her a "Nazi." The pro-Russian activists often threw such accusations to the address of the Ukrainians. They were initiated and spread by the Russian media.

At that time, Dunja Mijatovic held a meeting with journalists at the hotel, who told her about the situation with freedom of speech on the peninsula. A reporter from the Russian ORT TV channel also attended the meeting, but she kept silent throughout the meeting.

Symbolically, during this meeting, the work of journalists was blocked in Feodosia. According to the Information Resistance team, Ukrainian and foreign journalists were not allowed by the Russian Cossacks and military men to the territory of the Ukrainian Feodosia battalion of marines, which was blocked by the Russians. This resolution was allegedly passed by one of the Russian military leaders.

> "The "self-defense" representatives caught me and promised to kill me if I make at least one more shot. I was saved by my teammate, who delivered me from the hands of the "self-defense". They wanted to take away my camera, but they failed."

The photographer of Arguments of the Week. Crimea newspaper, **Stas Yurchenko**, came to a meeting right from the campaign "Women for Peace" held near the headquarters of the coastal defense of the Naval Forces of Ukraine at Karl Marx Street. There were clashes, provoked by people in camouflage with St. George ribbons, the fighters of the so-called "self-defense of Crimea".

"I went to the side, he said, but the "self-defense" representatives caught me and promised to kill me if I make at least one more shot. I was saved by my teammate, who delivered me from the hands of the "self-defense". They wanted to take away my camera, but they failed."

"I thought then, he says today, *that Dunja did not quite realize the danger of the conditions in which we are forced to work. When the meeting ended, I saw a crowd of protesters in the street who had been keeping the posters offering Barak Obama to "go home." I do not know how Obama is related to Dunja."*

> "When she was filming a military man with a machine gun, an unknown tall man, about one hundred and eighty centimeters high, hit her on the head from behind, took away her camera and fled."

At the meeting with Dunja Mijatovic, journalists said that conflicts occurred more and more often. A journalist from Sevastopol, a director of the IRS-Sevastopol Media Center **Tetiana Rykhtun**, said that she was attacked while working near the headquarters of the Navy of Ukraine, which was blocked by soldiers with no identifying tag. When Tetiana was filming a soldier with a machine gun, an unknown tall man, about one hundred and eighty centimeters high, hit her on the head from behind, took away her camera and fled. She did not know whether he was one of the so-called "self-defense of Crimea."

The meeting ended early, immediately after chanting from the crowd was heard from the street. The mission employees quickly accompanied Tetiana to another exit.

"The meeting was actually disrupted, recalls the editor in chief of the Center for Journalistic Investigations news agency, **Valentyna Samar**, *since a crowd of old ladies with posters against Obama and NATO was brought to the hotel main entrance. They rallied somewhere around the square, and they were brought to Dunja Mijatovic to disrupt the meeting with journalists.*

Dunja and her colleagues went to the backyard of the hotel, where their minibus was parked. The exit was blocked by several cars. There they also saw "self-defense" representatives, who were commanded by the classmate and right hand of Aksionov, Mykhailo Sheremet, who gave orders through a loudspeaker. After the annexation, he became the "deputy prime minister" of Crimea, and now he is a "deputy" of the Russian State Duma.

He was accompanied by a man, not from Crimea, who saw me and said, "Oh, Valentyna, I watched you on TV yesterday." Perhaps he was from the FSB or Russian Military Intelligence.

Sheremet and that man spoke with Dunja politely but firmly. They said that she should go to the airport and leave immediately. Some of their cars accompanied Dunja and her office staff; in fact, it was a convoy of the "self-defense" representatives.

We also followed them and accompanied them together with our Sevastopol peer, Tetiana Rykhtun, up to waiting hall to make sure that Dunja was safe."

A few hours later, it was announced that a special envoy of the UN Secretary General, **Robert Serry**, left Simferopol on the first available plane. In his memoirs, which he sent via e-mail, Mr. Serry stresses that he had no special envoy status at that time, like in other conflict situations requiring a decision and mandate from the Security Council. Russia in the UN Security Council objected to such a mission.

UN Secretary General, sending him to Crimea, was acting under Article 99 of the UN Charter, which allows him to *"...bring to the attention of the Security Council any matter which in his opinion may threaten the maintenance of international peace and security."*

Robert Serry In 2014 special envoy of the UN Sec-retary General. He arrived to Crimea during the occupation. The so colled self defence of Crimea made him to fly away. The picture is from his archive.

Robert Serry stresses that the role of the media in that situation was key for several reasons. As soon as the world learned about what was happening, it, according to Mr. Serry, ensured his personal security, and allowed him to draw the world's attention to the dangerous situation in Crimea.

"We tried to meet with the "prime minister" Aksionov, nominated without Kyiv's approval, recalls Robert Serry, *but he kept us waiting for almost an hour. I did meet on that day with representatives of the Russian community, Crimean authorities still loyal to Ukraine and the Tatar leader Chubarov.*

I remember receiving a call from acting Foreign Minister Oliferov early in the afternoon, suggesting I should try to visit the besieged Ukrainian admiralty in Simferopol if I could. As it was in my remit to talk with all parties concerned we included to go there at the end of the afternoon before going back to the hotel, where a press conference was scheduled.

Upon arrival at the admiralty we found the entry barricaded and green men patrolling the street. We managed to get inside, where I received a 45-minute briefing from the brave Commander (don't recall his name) describing to me a pretty desperate picture of Ukrainian naval forces across the peninsula, including his own condition (surrounded already for days).

After I came out of the admiralty, together with a UN colleague from New York and Vadim Kastelli (my interpreter), we were stopped by a group of armed green camouflaged men wearing no insignia, barking in Russian to us that they received "orders" to deport us directly to the airport of Simferopol.

They refused to identify themselves or disclose who had given these orders. We were also not allowed to go back to the hotel and pick up our bags. Refusing to go with them we managed to get inside our car – a white minibus only a few meters away. However, our way out was blocked by at least four black Landrovers.

The standoff lasted for several minutes. During that time I tried to reach the Deputy SG, Jan Eliasson (at the time also sent to Kyiv) and UN Security in New York; my colleagues were trying to reach out to Kyiv authorities and the press.

The standoff ended with our local driver threatened and opening the car doors. He was dragged out of the car and replaced by a green driver, while at the same time two armed men heaved themselves on the back chairs behind us.

Pro-Russian rally in Simferopol. Photo by Yuriy Lukanov.

Realising we were about to be deported, I pushed my colleague out of the side door and we began to walk away from the car (we lost Vadim who was sitting in front of the car). The green men followed, but did not try to stop us physically. This is how we ended up in a cafe in the Rosa Luxemburg street nearby. The green men stayed outside, guarding the door.

Inside the cafe we continued alerting New York and Kyiv to what happened, including the press waiting for us in the hotel! We were much relieved when one ITV crew managed to get inside the cafe (still wondering how) and began to interview me in a live broadcast. In the meantime a crowd was gathering in front of the cafe, shouting "Crimea... Russia!"

Through two pro-Ukrainian parliamentarians in Crimea I began negotiating a safe passage to the airport, realising the danger of further escalation and satisfied that at least the world knew (thanks to the press!) what was happening.

In the end I left the cafe through an angry mob to our mini-bus ready to take us to the airport (and of course escorted by green men in their own cars). Tickets had been reserved for us to take the last evening flight to

Istanbul (remember CNN "Breaking News" interview with Wolf Blitzer after arrival).

The following day I returned to Kyiv to resume my mission. That same evening Jan Eliasson and I were giving a video-briefing from Kyiv to the Security Council meeting in closed session. While all ambassadors expressed their relief that I had returned safely from Crimea, I remember Russian ambassador Vitaliy Churkin saying drily that he was also satisfied that I returned from „a somewhat complicated mission from Crimea."

> "It was the beginning of Crimea being stripped of unwanted witnesses of the Russian military raid to seize the peninsula, namely independent journalists and international observers."

The leader of the Center for Journalistic Investigations Valentyna Samar believes that the aggression with respect to Dunja Mijatovic and Robert Serry showed the true face of the Russian authorities, which did not want the world to learn what was happening in Crimea.

"These events were extremely important in the occupation of Crimea by Russia, says Valentyna Samar. It was the beginning of Crimea being stripped of unwanted witnesses of the Russian military raid to seize the peninsula, namely independent journalists and international observers. The fact that such brutal actions were committed in respect to representatives of key international institutions, the UN and the OSCE, also aimed at intimidating foreign journalists and diplomats. Everyone had to think that if the representatives of the OSCE and the UN had been treated in such a way, one could only imagine what would be done with people of a lower rank. Indeed, the journalists were "extinguished" indiscriminately, beaten, equipment was confiscated, and filming was prevented.

Such actions of the puppeteers of the "self-defense representatives" (according to the investigation conducted by our peers from the Russian Novaya Gazeta, during the raid of the Russian Federation, the people of the chairman of the Committee on Information Policy of the State Duma of Russia Leonid Levin and Aleksandr Boroday, who later became the head of the government of the so-called „Donetsk People's Republic" were in charge of the media) were a well-thought tactics. It was intended to discourage journalists to go to Crimea in order to film, describe and monitor what was happening there actually. At the time of the so-called "referendum", only the "insider" journalists and "observers", Russian or those from the post-Soviet countries, as well as bribed "foreign observers" from Europe were to stay in Crimea."

Subsequent events have confirmed that they struggle with the media systemically and in a variety of ways, namely restrict access to information, intimidate and arrest the journalists, brutally beat people with press cards, do not allow international observers to work, and use other means. Events after the annexation have shown that they are not going to abandon this policy.

On March 7, Dunja Mijatovic held a press conference in Kyiv. She did not speak about the attitude of the representatives of the so-called "self-defense" to her. She gave only a general assessment of the situation with freedom of speech in the region. She noted that in Crimea *"access to official information from the local government is provided to loyal journalists only."*

Moreover, Mijatovic said, *"I am extremely concerned about the situation with freedom of speech; every day we see the intimidation, beatings and censorship of the media. I urge all those responsible to stop the information war, to guarantee the safety of journalists in and outside Crimea, and to start immediately the de-escalation of the situation, allowing the media to cover the events freely."*

Two years later, Dunja Mijatovic again personally experienced the Russian way of doing business in Crimea. After a search of the journalist Mykola Semena and bringing charges against him on April 19, 2016, Independent Media Trade Union of Ukraine and the National Union of Journalists of Ukraine at the congress of the European Federation of Journalists in Sarajevo urged her to organize an international mission monitoring the freedom of expression in Crimea. She said she was working on this idea.

On May 31, 2016, in her office in Vienna, Mijatovic announced[1] the launch of work on the creation of a special international mission

---

1   OSCE special mission for the rights of journalists in Crimea will be created / Detector. Media, 5.31.2016. URL: http://detector.media/infospace/article/115594/2016-05-31-obse-stvorit-spetsialnu-misiyu-shchodo-prav-zhurnalistiv-u-krimu/

for journalists' rights. The Deputy Secretary General of the International Federation of Journalists **Jeremy Dear** said that the federation is *"highly interested in creating a mission to solve the problems associated with the rights of journalists in Crimea."*

Anti-Ukrainian and anti-Western leaflets in Simferopol. "West, do not stick your nose in the Crimean question" is written on one of them.
Photo by Yuriy Lukanov.

However, the mission never took place. No official explanation was provided. The lobby knows that the Russian government refused to provide the mission with access to Crimea.

Bloody Fight in Sevastopol

Ten days before the illegal "referendum" on the status of Crimea, a mass beating of journalists occurred in Sevastopol. The cameraman of Inter TV channel, **Volodymyr Diedov** had a rib broken, which struck the lung. He was operated on.

Andriy Tsaplienko, a TV journalist known for his work in hot spots, had six ribs broken. He said he had worked in hot spots in many countries, but never thought that this would happen in the territory of his native country.

A Greek journalist **Kostas Onisenko** had his nose broken. These are just a few examples. There were many more injured journalists.

The then reporter of the Inter TV channel, a native of Crimea **Olena Mekhanik** says that she was not affected physically, but killed morally. And today, when she recalls the events of that day, tears appear in her eyes and her hands begin to tremble.

"A week before the beating, I was filming Ukrainian marines. In front of the military unit, people gathered for a pro-Russian rally. They tried not to let us in the military unit, and objected to filming the real situation.

At that time, all Crimean and Russian media already disseminated information that ninety percent of the Crimean military units laid down their arms and sided with the Russian puppet Aksionov.

> "The main reason for the beating was a desire to intimidate journalists. Not just us. All those who worked on the peninsula and who covered the events."

We started visiting the military units and witnessed that it was not true, and Ukrainian soldiers did not intend to lay down their weapons. They called us and asked us to come in and tell how they live in the siege and under pressure. Every day, my peers and I filmed reports from other military units.

After that, people from the so-called "people's self-defense" with St. George ribbons started meeting us near the military units and tried to prevent us getting in. They sought to prevent the spread of information denying the Russian propaganda.

Olena Mekhanik at work in Crimea. Photo from her archive.

So, the main reason for the beating was a desire to intimidate journalists. Not just us. All those who worked on the peninsula and who covered the events. Apparently, the beating organizers hoped that our peers from different countries would learn about it and stop their activity.

On the eve of the beating, we were warned that it was very dangerous to work in Sevastopol, since all taxi drivers in the city were equipped with radios and tracked the movement of all film teams about the city. I did not understand at that time where this information was passed on. I just did not take notice of it.

Perhaps it was a mistake. Perhaps, if we were more careful and cautious, that what happened would not have happened. It is now clear that the taxi drivers were spying in favor of Russian and pro-Russian organizations.

Late at night on March 7, I was shooting a news story in the air defense unit in Sevastopol. I was filming military women. After shooting, late at night, we left the unit, but managed to pass just two hundred meters. The soldiers called me and said that the assault began, the Russian military machines were ramming the gate.

"Perhaps they realized that journalists had filmed this crime and then started beating everyone who had professional devices. They beat very severely. It was clear that these people knew how to beat and how to bully."

I began to call reporters and asked them to come to the unit. We came back and started filming. Gradually, journalists of different media came. Around fifteen reporters and cameramen gathered.

Suddenly people in several cars, of athletic build, wearing masks, arrived. Some of them wore camouflage, others tracksuits. These people, there were about ten of them, dissolved in the crowd. First, they wondered what was happening.

Perhaps they realized that journalists had filmed this crime and then started beating everyone who had professional devices. They beat very severely. It was clear that these people knew how to beat and how to bully.

I stopped in my tracks with fear. When these people moved towards me, the Greek journalist Kostas Onisenko, who was with us, rescued me from being beaten, or maybe even from death. He pushed me into the car. We got in the cars indiscriminately, choosing the closest one. We were six in one car. Besides me, there was the driver of the Crimean bureau of Inter channel, Serhiy Shchuryk, the Greek journalist Kostas Onisenko, special reporter of Inter Andriy Tsaplienko, and Inter cameramen, Volodymyr Diedov and Pavlo Lysenko.

We started the car immediately, because one of the attackers rushed at us.

I started calling reporters and saying, "Do not come here, because they beat everyone." I managed to make some calls. We were caught up. Our car was cut off. They ran up to us and opened the door on my side. I was sitting in the back sea, holding a camera in my hands. They snatched my camera and started hitting it against the door of the car. Then they finally broke this camera against asphalt.

Our driver miraculously managed to bypass this devil crowd. I was called by Savik Shuster studio. They said that they were going to have a live stream with me. I only had time to say that we were being chased and managed to hide the phone.

Then we were surrounded by several cars, I guess three. The same people, who were near of air defense unit, got out of them.

Something terrible has started. They beat the car first, then they opened all the doors. My peer, Andriy Tsaplienko, tried to start some negotiations with them. It did not make sense. They cried out "Face down!

Hands behind your head!" They started shooting. They all had guns and fired into the air.

They pulled the boys out of the car and threw them to the ground. They beat them fiercely. This was accompanied by terrible cries. They shouted "Welcome to Sevastopol," "It is Sevastopol, baby!" and so on. I will omit obscene words.

The Greek journalist had his nose broken. He was lying in a pool of blood. Our cameraman was beaten in the face. They beat indiscriminately. There was a mess. I sat in the back seat, staring at it in shock.

One of the attackers continuously got in the car, grabbed anything he saw, shook the rugs, seized flash cards, wires, equipment, phones, any media.

They grabbed my bag, and began shaking it. They found chevrons. I did a series of stories from military units, and Ukrainian soldiers gave me chevrons as a souvenir. They provoked a furious rage of attackers. They poked the chevrons in my face and cried "Why do you need it? What is it?" I tried to explain to them. But they were furious. They did not want to listen.

They emptied my wallet. They searched for SIM cards, memory cards. Meanwhile, I had a lot of discount cards in my wallet, like any woman going to the shops. One outraged man poked the wallet in my face, "Why do you have so many cards?" I said "Because I go shopping." He scattered everything around violently. It seems that anything could cause their wild irritation.

They took my passport. When they saw that I had a Crimean registration, then began to show it to each other, calling me treacherous. The look away the guys' passports and said that now they knew where we lived, and where our families lived. It sounded like a threat. They never returned the documents.

They beat the cameraman, Volodymyr Diedov, the most, although he was short and the most defenseless. He tried to hide his head into the car. I grabbed him with my hands and asked them not to beat him on the head. One of the attackers simply removed my hands and hit him four times so hard that I thought that this was the end for him.

Two guys, cameraman Volodymyr Diedov and Greek journalist Kostas Onisenko, were put into the trunk of our car by force and began firing. I was sitting on the back seat and did not see what was happening *behind. I heard they put them there. I thought that they were shooting at the trunk. It was very scary.*

I do not know why, but they allowed us to leave in half an hour.

At the checkpoint on the outskirts of Sevastopol we were stopped. There were a few dozen people, Cossacks, military man, and traffic cops. I saw a man in a police uniform and went towards him. I wanted to ask for help.

When I approached the policeman, he looked at me with a sarcastic smile. I realized that they knew everything. They are on the same side as the assailants. They switched to serve the enemy.

The police again searched our car. They looked at us with a crooked smile and mockingly asked: "What happened to you? Where are you from?"

I was approached by a man (and it was the eve of March 8, International Women's Day) who said, "Congratulations of March the eighth!" I asked, "Are you kidding?" He answered, "No. This is our congratulation on Women's Day."

At the hospital, the doctors did not find any serious injury of our guys. It was the Simferopol City Emergency Hospital No. 6. The doctors behaved as if they were warned that the beaten television employees, and they don't have to care of them. Only in Kyiv, it became obvious that the guys got injured seriously.

At the hospital, I gave to Andriy Tsaplienko a GoPro camera, by which I managed to film the attack on a military unit and the start of the slaughter in Sevastopol. I miraculously did not lose my head and managed to hide the camera under my clothes as soon as I realized that they would take everything away. All the time, I was dreadfully afraid that it would be found. Then we were able to use this priceless video in our materials.

When I arrived at my mother's, who lives in Simferopol, it appeared that she had watched the TV and had seen everything that had happened. She was as shocked as I was. We didn't fall asleep until morning. That night we first realized the scale of the disaster and tried to figure out what to do next.

In the morning, three people called me, one by one. They gave only their names, not organizations or whom they represented.

The latter said he was ready to provide help to me. He said he would hide me in a safe place, that I should not be afraid of anything, but I should go out and talk. I guess these were some provocateurs.

So I decided to leave the peninsula immediately.

Currently I am working as an editor in chief of the Radio Svoboda project, "Donbas. Realities."

Victims of the attack returned to Kyiv. Photo courtesy of Pavlo Lysenko.

The reporter of Inter TV channel, **Roman Bochkala,** received the records of intercepted radio communication of the attackers at the frequency of 446 MHz from the Ukrainian Navy officers in Sevastopol. It was proof that the attack was not accidental; it was a well-coordinated campaign to destroy the video of an attack on a military unit.

A military man with a concealed face for security reasons told reporters on Skype that there is a radio channel called "Autokanal" in Sevastopol. According to him, this "Autokanal" was used by the groups of the so-called "self-defense". This frequency was also used by Sevastopol taxi drivers, whose cars were chasing Inter journalists. According to Ukrainian soldiers, this campaign was coordinated by some intelligence agencies, probably Russian military intelligence. The coordinator with the alias Moskva had a Russian vehicle plate number, as was reported by him in one of the radio communications.

Here are some excerpts from radio communications:

*"- Who was at Kotovskogo? (Street name – ed.). Intercepting down, guys,
move on.
- Renault location?"
"- Kill the camera! Just block!
- The reason for stopping?
- Inter TV channel. Destroy the material. Just block and hold. We are com-
ing."
"- Breaker, are you by! The combat group, what to do with Renault? What's
the task?
- Start hitting it there.
- Check the cassettes, they might have dropped them all in the cabin. And
find all sticks."
Video posted on YouTube on March 12, 2014.*

Russians Only

Shortly before the above events, on February 28, 2014, the author of
this book went to the Crimean Parliament building at Karl Marx
Street, since it became known that Russian troops who occupied
government buildings went out to the street. The quarter was surrounded by the so-called "self-defense of Crimea", which consisted
of young civilians. I showed the press card. I was not let in.

I stepped aside and stood by the TV crews, a journalist and a
cameraman of the TV channel. They filmed what was happening
behind a "self-defense" chain. I also photographed the servicemen,
who were seen clearly. Suddenly a man approached the TV workers and said, *"Come along."*

The "self-defense" made way for the TV workers, and they
moved towards the Parliament. I went with them. The man leading
us probably thought that I was a member of their team and therefore did not object.

Near the Verkhovna Rada, a woman of retirement age, one of
those catered the "self-defense" at a special table, came up to me.

"Warm drinks to journalists, she said and poured tea from a
thermos into a disposable cup. *Tell Putin to destroy all this opposition,
like Nemtsov. Our Yanukovych did not do that, and you see what happened."*

She obviously took me for a Russian journalist, since the others just could not be there.

"Self-defense of Crimea" in Simferopol. Photo by Yuriy Lukanov.

About one hundred and fifty meters away from the Parliament building, there was a car with the inscription "Mir International TV and Radio Company" in Russian. It was a machine for video and audio broadcasting on air or to the editor.

It served exclusively Russian journalists. This single machine worked for the TV stations, which allegedly were considered competitive. This fact testified that everything was organized so that only the Russians had access to exclusive information. The deputies of the Crimean Parliament came to Russian journalists. They, in turn, had access to the Parliament premises. The only journalists I saw there were Russian.

The next day, on March 1, according to the[2] Mass Information Institute in Simferopol, unidentified masked persons did not allow

2   ATR crew not allowed to the press conference in the occupied Council of Ministers in Crimea / Mass Information Institute, 01.03.2014.URL: http://imi.org.ua/news/znimalnu-grupu-atr-ne-pustili-na-pres-konferentsiyu-u-zahopleniy-radi-ministriv-krimu/

ATR camera crew to a press conference in the occupied Council of Ministers of Crimea, while Russian media got in the Council without interference.

"Before that, – says the news – a man who introduced himself as the Deputy Chairman of the Board came out to the media and said that today a government meeting would be held, after which a press conference was scheduled. According to him, the journalists were working in the building already. The reporters of the Tatar ATR Channel were not allowed to the building of the Council of Ministers, while the Russian media got to the Council without interference."

ATR journalists, in Zaman program, stated that they connected this position to attempts of the press conference organizers to present the events in the light favorable for the Russian TV channels. As an example of manipulations, they cited the story of the Russia 24 channel, which stated that the Crimean Tatars beat peaceful protesters who defended Crimea's accession to Russia. It was stressed that 30 people were injured, and some were in serious condition. Russia 24 journalists used the video of clashes in Kyiv, which recorded the beating of protesters by "Berkut."

Also, as ATR reported[3], the representatives of the "Crimean front", wearing masks, promised to hold their own press conference. Before that, they closed themselves in the building in the House of Trade Unions in Simferopol, where the Center for Investigative Reporting was located.

On March 6, Ukrainian and foreign journalists again were not allowed in the building of the Crimean Parliament for an extraordinary meeting, where the decision on "Crimea's accession to Russia" and "referendum" was made.

In addition, only Russian journalists were allowed for a briefing by the head of the Crimean Parliament, Volodymyr Konstantinov.

---

3   ATR crew not allowed to the press conference in the occupied Council of Ministers in Crimea / Mass Information Institute, 01.03.2014. URL: http://imi. org.ua/news/znimalnu-grupu-atr-ne-pustili-na-pres-konferentsiyu-u-zahople niy-radi-ministriv-krimu /

"Self-defense of Crimea" blocks military unit in Simferopol.
Photo by Yuriy Lukanov.

The journalists of the leading Ukrainian news agencies, TV channels and their peers from France, Italy, Great Britain and several other countries were not allowed into the building of the Crimean Parliament and had to rest content with comments of some deputies who left the premises of the Crimean Parliament.

Limited "referendum"

On March 12, 2014, the Supreme Council of Crimea reported that by March 13 the journalists shall get accredited to cover the "referendum", which was scheduled for March 16. Particularly notable was the fact that the journalists faced a number of requirements, including the refusal to spread "negative": "...*The journalist shall objectively inform its media audience about the voting, use the documented facts in their operations, comply with journalistic ethics, and not distribute negative materials.*"

The lawyer of the Media Law Institute, Ihor Rozkladay, commenting on[4] this fact for Telekrytyka, criticized the requirement for journalists "not to distribute negative materials," because "negative" is a value judgment, the dissemination of which, according to a lawyer, is not the ground for deprivation of accreditation.

He stressed that the said accreditation procedure contradicts the Ukrainian legislation and is generally illegitimate. *"Given that the Crimean "referendum" is illegitimate, everything that happens in its context cannot be legitimate either,"* he said.

Besides, the journalists were requested to provide a number of documents for accreditation:

"The application must be accompanied by:

- *a stamped copy of the certificate of the media state registration or a copy of the broadcasting license of the audiovisual media;*
- *full name of the media, its founder or publishers, editorial board location, coverage area, business phone and fax numbers, full name of the media manager, and a contact telephone number;*
- *full name, position, passport details (number, series, issuing authority and date of issue), contact telephone number of the media journalist being accredited;*
- *technical equipment to be used by the journalist of the accredited media to perform its professional duties."*

---

4   In Crimea, the procedure of media accreditation for the "referendum" was announced; it contradicts Ukrainian laws / Telekrytyka, 11.03.2014. URL: http://ua.telekritika.ua/pravo/2014-03-12/91379

Crimean Tatars protest against the so-called «referendum» in Simferopol. The billboardsays: "Together with Russia. On March 16—referendum".
Photo by Yuriy Lukanov.

"The accreditation application submitted in violation of this procedure shall be rejected," said the Verkhovna Rada of Crimea.

"In one day, such requirements could be fulfilled by the local media only, and only provided that they put everything aside and start collecting documents, said the director of the Center for Investigative Reporting **Valentyna Samar**. *Non-Crimean publications were not physically capable of such a step; they wouldn't manage to deliver the stamped documents by regular mail overnight. The list was prepared so that only "insider" journalists loyal to Russia could get to the "referendum.""*

However, the presence or the absence of accreditation did not play a special role, since the journalists, as the then Radio Liberty reporter in Crimea **Volodymyr Prytula** says, could be rejected on the way to the polls of the so-called "referendum for the independence of Crimea." According to him, the steps were taken to minimize the number of journalists getting to the polls.

"Without accreditation for the "referendum," he says, I could go to my polling station as a voter. It was located at Shchorsa Street. However, the so-called "self-defense" representatives were on duty near each poll and

inside. They fixed everything that was happening. They knew me in person.

As soon as I pulled out my camera, they immediately asked me:

> *- Who are you?*
> *- I am a journalist.*
> *- Do you have accreditation? On what basis are you filming?*
> *- I have a certificate.*
> *- You may not film here without accreditation.*

We could only shoot from the outside, from a distance."

The then director of the Kerch editorial department of Arguments of the Week. Kerch **Olena Yurchenko** says that as soon as she tried to film the so-called "referendum" on a poll in Kerch, she was immediately saw off the premises.

"I tried to shoot one of the Kerch polls, tells Olena Yurchenko. Some young men immediately came up to me and wanted to detain me, because I was filming without permission. I saw one friend and pretended to be focused on him, waved and went towards him. They did not detain me.

After that, we toured about all stations. We left the car around the corner. I went to the station and watched how many people were there, how many ballots were in the ballot boxes and the like. By the way, there were very few people. I visited polling stations during elections, so I can compare. Attendance at the so-called "referendum" was 20 percent of the normal.

Toward the afternoon, I learned that foreign observers would come to the polling station at a high school at Lenin Square. I took the camera and went there to watch.

The observers were accompanied by the then director of the press service of the city executive committee, Olha Arkhypenko, and the journalists of the media loyal to Russia. I asked Olha to let me in too.

She gave an order. I managed to make a few shots only. I was asked again "Who are you? On what grounds do you work?" I had to leave."

ATR TV channel reporter, **Shevket Namatullaev,** while covering the "referendum" was attacked by unknown persons. He says he came to the polling station in the Kamenka neighborhood of Simferopol.

Journalists are working in Crimea. Photo by Stanislav Yurchenko (RFE/RL)

"We arrived at six pm, says Shevket, two hours before the end of the so-called "referendum". The polling station was located in the House of Culture. The cameraman and I showed our license. The members of the station commission did not object to our shooting.

There was nobody in the station. The ballots barely covered the bottom of the ballot boxes. To our question, the election commission members said they around fifty percent of registered voters voted. A total number of voters, according to them, was one thousand eighteen hundred people.

I expressed doubt that in this case there would be around nine hundred ballots in the ballot boxes, and they are obviously not so many. Then they said that thirty percent of the voters arrived.

At eight o'clock in the evening, the voting ends and the commission chairman tells us to leave, because they need to count the votes. I disagree and explain that we have the right to attend the calculation.

The commission chairman calls the head of the so-called "Central Election Commission", Mikhail Malyshev. She explains the situation, then passes the telephone to me, and I present my arguments with reference to the Voting Regulation. He agrees that we do have the right to stay.

"While the car was moving, four masked men with machine guns jumped out of it. They command us to leave, and forced us to put our hands on the hood. We explained that we are journalists filming the "referendum"."

When the vote counting began, I saw that they violated the Voting Regulation. They did not destroy unused ballots, and began to count them. There was about one hundred and sixty or one hundred and seventy ballots.

Voting during the so-called "referendum" on the status of Crimea.
Photo by Stanislav Yurchenko (RFE/RL)

I say that they violated the Regulation, and should first destroy the unused ballots. They ask, "Who cares?" I emphasize that it is stipulated by the Regulation. The commission members say they made a mistake because of us, because we distracted them. All this was happening live.

When they, as a whole cavalcade of six cars, went to the so-called Central Election Commission to deliver the ballots, we followed them. Suddenly, we were pushed to the curb by an offroadster. We decided to stay for a while and proceed.

Suddenly, another offroadster arrives. They press us and commanded us to stop from the window.

While the car was moving, four masked men with machine guns jumped out of it. They command us to leave, and forced us to put our hands on the hood. We explained that we are journalists filming the "referendum". I show my certificate. They request a passport. I say I have no passport.

They request to show our camera to see what we shot. However, the cameraman, having seen that we were chased, threw the memory card under the rug of our car. We say that everything was broadcast live, so we have no record. They detained us for ten minutes and then released us.

I assume that the ballot commission members called somewhere and asked them to detain us. They had to count all ballots, because only ten percent of voters voted, while they needed sixty or seventy percent. They have neutralized us, and added these ballots.

Our colleagues reported that this happened everywhere. So I have no doubt that the so-called "referendum" was a sham.

We were not allowed to attend the approval of the "referendum" results by the so-called "Central Election Commission." The press service director said openly that the Russian media only would be allowed."

Accused of spying

On March 13, 2014, three days before the "referendum", ATR TV channel delivered the news that on Konteynerna street the „"self-defense" captured a cameraman of the French Channel+ **David Geoffrey** who was filming the seizure of the lubricant base. He managed to throw the camera over the fence to his peer reporter, but he did not have time to climb himself, he was pulled down by the "self-defense".

At that time, the author of this book was at the Center for Investigative Reporting. I and two Center journalists, **Serhiy Mokrushyn** and **Yevhen Harkusha**, got in the editorial car and decided to try to release our French colleague.

> "Russia really wanted to pretend that the "people of Crimea" themselves wanted to get under its wing, and journalists were showing that it is far from being so. Therefore, they had to be neutralized."

"We arrived at the entrance to the lubricant base, says **Serhiy Mokrushyn**. *We met a twenty-two year old guy in camouflage jacket and jogging trousers. We asked why he had stopped us. The guy replied that the base is controlled by the "Army of Crimea." According to him, on the*

eve, Prime Minister Aksionov declared that "self-defense" is now the "Army of Crimea."

We explained why we arrived, and he called the "commander." A man around forty years old came and said they could give us the journalist in exchange for a flash card with his video. We promised to do it.

We went to the next street, and called the ATR channel, where the French colleague of the detained cameraman was staying. We asked them to give us a flash card with footage shot by the detained cameraman. We got it in half an hour.

We again contacted the "commander" and showed the stick.

> *- Is that all? – he asked,*
> *- No. We need the footage from all journalists who were filming here.*
> *- How do we know who was filming here? – we asked, it is simply impossible.*
> *- Well, you know your guys. Otherwise, no exchange will occur."*

We continued negotiations with a gray fifty-year-old man, who called himself morale officer Stanislav Selivanov. He said that the Frenchman would be tried for espionage. I was curious:

> *- Under which law?*
> *- We will work it out.*

Having learned that I am from Kyiv, he refused to talk, because he did not trust the "false Ukrainian media." However, he continued negotiations with the Crimeans.

Through my peers in Kyiv, I reported on the situation to the International Federation of Journalists and the Union of Journalists of Russia. I asked them to intervene. I sent them Selivanov's and the "Crimean government" phone numbers, asking to put pressure on them.

The European Federation of Journalists responded immediately. Its Secretary General Ricardo Gutierrez called, asked about the situation and promised to take action. I suggested that he put pressure the "Crimean government" through the European Parliament.

The negotiations, breaks and new talks lasted for about four hours. Finally, they called my Crimean colleagues and invited them to another meeting, implying that they were going to release David Geoffrey.

"Political officer" Stanislav Selivanov said again that he would not communicate with Ukrainian journalists and asked the Crimeans to come up.

Crimean photojournalists during the mourning rally of the Crimean Tatars on May 18, 2014. Photo by Stanislav Yurchenko (RFE/RL)

We went towards him; there were several people, including a French cameraman and an interpreter. Selivanov asked David Geoffrey to confirm that he was treated properly, was not beaten, and his scratched hand was bandaged. He confirmed and pulled a sandwich wrapped in cloth out of his pocket to show that he was fed carefully.

When we approached the car, the Frenchman refused to get it. He said that he did not know who we were, so he did not trust us. We called the ATR, where his colleague was staying, and asked to assure him that we have good intentions. They talked, and David get in the car with us. His phone was seized until the next day, as they said, for verification.

"It was not the first illegal detention of a journalist, says Mokrushyn. I have no doubt that the "self-defense" has been instructed to counter, beat, detain, and intimidate journalists so that they no longer had a desire to talk about the Russian occupation of the peninsula. Russia really wanted to pretend that the "people of Crimea" themselves wanted to get under its wing, and journalists were showing that it is far from being so. Therefore, they had to be neutralized."

On May 28, 2014, the website of Berdyansk, Zaporizhzhia region, Berdyansk.Biz wrote an article[5] on local separatists. It published a photo with the character named Stanislav Selivanov, who looked very similar to the one who led negotiations in Simferopol on the captured French journalist.

At the time of publication, according to the publication, Selivanov was a commandant of separatists in Anthracite, Luhansk region, which was controlled by the so-called "Luhansk People's Republic" established after the Russian invasion of Eastern Ukraine.

He also ran for the mayor of Berdyansk in 2006. In 2008, Selivanov ran for the mayor of Kyiv. He lost in both cases.

Earlier, on February 5, 2009, the same edition published Selivanov's biography which he submitted as a candidate for mayor of Kyiv in 2008. According to it, from 1998 to 2004, he had been working at the State Administration of Krasnoyarsk region of Russia as the Governor Adviser.

According to Berdyansk.Biz, Selivanov said that he was close to the legendary Russian General Aleksandr Lebed, who had been the governor of Krasnoyarsk region from 1998 to 2002, until his death. The publication reveals it as a blatant lie. In particular, it refers to Krasnoyarsk journalists who claim that Lebed had no such adviser.

ORD website mentions in the 90s', Selivanov's surname was Hurtovyi, and he had a criminal record.

---

5   Berdyansk separatists participate in war (supplemented) / Berdyansk.Biz, 28.05.2014. URL: http://pro.berdyansk.biz/content.php?id=21914

The Security Service of Ukraine, at the request of the author of these lines, said that Stanislav Selivanov *"in December 2014, during preliminary investigation by investigators of the security agencies in the criminal proceedings was served a suspicion in absentia of committing the crimes under Part 2 of Article 110, Part 1 of Article 111, and Part 1 of Article 258-3 of the Criminal Code of Ukraine. Now he is hiding from the investigation."*

These articles are "Encroachment on the territorial integrity and inviolability of Ukraine," "Treason," "Creation of a terrorist group or a terrorist organization."

After the expansion of the aggression against Ukraine on February 24, 2022, Russia seized the city of Berdyansk in Zaporizhzhia region, where Selivanov had lived before the war in 2014 began. On April 21 the so-called military commandant of the city of Berdyansk—a Russian colonel Artyom Bardin released a decree regarding the appointment of the deputies of the so-called city mayor. Among them there was Stanislav Selivanov, who was supposed to be responsible for the social matters.

Later, on September 6, Bardin's car was blown up by the Ukrainian partisans. He later died in hospital from the injuries received.

The city of Berdyansk is situated on the Sea of Azov shores, 200 kilometers away from the regional center—Zaporizhzhia. This city was highly important for the Ukrainian economics, since there was a functioning seaport, through which the significant volumes of the metallurgical and agricultural products were transported.

Besides that, it was a popular resort with a 20 km shoreline with beaches. Right now, they are deserted.

On May 25, on the website "Primorka.city" which was not under control of the occupants, it was told about the summer season, which was being disrupted. Since the vacationers were the source of income for the majority of Berdyansk citizens, the disruption of the season led to the impoverishment of the inhabitants.

On September 7, 2022, The Security Service of Ukraine declared the suspicion to six collaborators, among which Stanislav Selivanov was listed: *"Another collaborator — Stanislav Selivanov is one of the founders of "Putin's Political Party" in Ukraine and he has been actively cooperating with enemy since 2014. The resident of the city of Berdyansk took active part in the annexation of the Crimean Peninsula and was awarded with a medal „for the returning of Crimea". Later he held a position of a member of the "Council of DPR".* After the occupation of the part of Zaporizhzhia region, he was "promoted" and appointed „deputy mayor of Berdyansk on social matters".

Just like other traitors, he will face up to 15 years in prison.

The son was held responsible for his father

On March 16, 2014, on the day of the so-called "referendum", a Crimean by origin, documentary film cameraman **Yaroslav Pilunskiy**, and his colleague, a citizen of Russia **Yuriy Gruzinov** disappeared in Crimea. The alarm was rang by family, friends and colleagues from the cinema association Babylon`13 formed when shooting the events at Euromaidan, of which both missing men were members.

Six days later, Pilunskiy and Gruzinov emerged from obscurity. It turned out that they were sitting "in the basement" controlled by the so-called "Crimean self-defense."

"We were filming everything that happened at Maidan, says Pilunskiy. We have made "The First Hundred" documentary. Naturally, when the events in Crimea began to develop, Yuriy Gruzinov and I decided to go there.

I am a native of Crimea. At that time, my father Leonid Pilunskiy was an MP of the Verkhovna Rada of Crimea, opposing the annexation. My family and I really care for the fate of Crimea.

Going there, we were going to somehow convey the truth about what happened on the Maidan to the local people.

We entered Crimea on March 4. When we arrived, I realized that it was too late. Masses of people were in such a twisted state of mind that they wouldn't perceive the information. We decided to film the seizure of the military units. That's what we did.

On the day of the pseudo referendum we learned that the voting was based on Russian passports. We started the morning with calling colleagues, collecting information. I guess we learned about it from ATR Channel journalists.

"We were laying overnight with our hands tied with duct tape and construction couplers. We had towels on our heads. We were in different chambers. I managed to loosen the ties on my hands, removed the bandage and looked around. The mattress on the floor where I was laying had traces of fresh blood and a hole similar to the bullet hole."

We went to the polling station at Studentska Street. It is on the outskirts of Simferopol. There are universities around. Since many foreigners, especially Russians, study there, we assumed that they vote based on non-Ukrainian passports.

Pro-Ukrainian picket in Simferopol. Photo by Stanislav Yurchenko (RFE/RL)

First we decided to enter and scout the situation. Yuriy said that he would take his GoPro camera, which is very small in size, just in case.

Yuriy made the mistake by starting to film right away. He was attacked and his hands were tied. I could not remain silent and began to intercede for him. I was tied too. These were local young men.

We were brought into the car, where a man about fifty years old was sitting, who told us, "Take on and I'll make a cripple of you." Then we were taken to the headquarters of the so-called "self-defense", the one near the Lenin monument in the city center. There were lots of Cossacks, clearly not Ukrainian.

We were questioned by some local people. They were obviously amateurs. They put some simple questions: "What are you doing? Why?" and the like. During interrogation, we agreed that they would release us. They even promised to return the camera, having retained the material.

During Yuriy's interrogation a man came, took my passport and saw my surname. He said, "Keep these Cossacks tight." He must have associated it with my father, a pro-Ukrainian Crimean Parliament Member. This is how the son was held liable for his father. Then they took our phones containing the numbers, for example, of the First Hundred centurion, indicating that this is a person from Maidan.

Then the professionals came. They were clearly from some special service. We were blindfolded, and put in handcuffs. They looked like the guys conquering Slovyansk. They put us into the Gazelle specifically prepared for this.

We did not see where we were brought, for our eyes were covered. However, I assume that it was the regional recruiting office. It is located next to the railway station. I heard the sound of trains from there.

We were laying overnight with our hands tied with duct tape and construction couplers. We had towels on our heads. We were in different chambers. I managed to loosen the ties on my hands, removed the bandage and looked around. The mattress on the floor where I was laying had traces of fresh blood and a hole similar to the bullet hole. I lifted the mattress and looked below it. There was no bullet trace on the floor. Perhaps, the mattress was simply torn. The tiled floor and walls of the warehouse were splashed with blood.

> "At some point, he pointed the gun at my temple and asked, „Do you feel what it is? I relaxed, for I did not expect the further hitting. I was not scared. I said, „"Yes, I feel." He was angry that I was not scared. Then, still pointing the gun at me, he says a brilliant phrase, „You are my enemy, because your camera is stronger than my arms."

A day later, young guys in ski masks came. One of them saw that I freed my hand and said, "Pull your arm once again and I'll make a cripple of you."

I was brought into the room. The conversation started with kicking me in the solar plexus, and then in the groin. However, after the first hit I fell down and managed to cover the groin. After that, they beat me with a metal tube on my head covered with a towel so that no trace was left.

They asked stupid questions, a complete set of delusion from the Russian TV. "When will the Right Sector come to Crimea? Why did you come to Maidan?" He looked behind my shirt and saw no cross there. "Are you a Jew?"

At some point, he pointed the gun at my temple and asked, "Do you feel what it is? I relaxed, for I did not expect the further hitting. I was not scared. I said, "Yes, I feel." He was angry that I was not scared. Then, still pointing the gun at me, he says a brilliant phrase, "You are my enemy, because your camera is stronger than my arms."

When they asked me "Why did you come to Maidan?", I answered "We came to the Maidan to remove criminality from power." He took the gun away from my temple and pointed it at my leg near the knee, "You won't deceive a man with two university degrees."

I saw that it seemed to them that they had caught spies. We were lucky because we were waiting for the Crimean "Berkut" which raged at Maidan. Therefore, we were not beaten as heavily as it could be.

We were given food only three days later. It was barley and stew.

We were not taken to the toilet. There was a plastic bottle for urine. When Mr. Brown was knocking on my back door, they took me out. There was a queue to the toilet. I had a loosely tied towel on my eyes, and I saw a guy, whose eyes were tied with a Ukrainian flag. This is how they abused people mentally.

There was no drain there, and the toilet was filled with shit. It was so ugly that then I ate twenty grams of barley so that not to fill the stomach and not want to go to the toilet.

While we were sitting, someone seized our car. It broke down and we delivered it to the service station. During the interrogation, I told them where it was. They came to that station. There was a day off. They broke the door and took the non-running car. Then this car had been standing at the parking lot of the Security Service of Ukraine in Simferopol for a few weeks.

They also seized our equipment. Having arrived in Crimea, we hired a local Crimean Tatar who was driving the car for us. Our main equipment remained in his car. After we were arrested, he behaved carelessly. He was asked by some traitor Crimean Tatars who used to serve in the Security Service of Ukraine, and then switched to the Federal Security Service, whether he would receive a Russian passport. He refused and argued strongly. Then he was searched and our equipment was found. They seized it with all the footage.

I was not allowed to call. My wife was calling continuously. I felt that it was her, and asked them to answer and say that I was alive. One of them picked up the phone, saw the "Honey" inscription and commented with a mocking smile that wives are not called like this.

> "It was a pure crime. Thuggish paramilitary structure. I understand that it had been prepared long before the Russians attacked Crimea. I use the following image: when you go to the bottom, then you fear, and when you reach the bottom, it is not scary any more, since from the bottom you can see the dangers above. So, we were in the bottom."

My wife called the Ministry of Defense of Russia. However, they said they knew nothing about those who had detained us.

The First Hundred of the Maidan, the movie about which I shot, advocated us. They asked the organization of ex-soldiers who fought in Afghanistan, "No one but us." This organization is spread across the former Soviet space, and includes people with different views. This allowed them to contact their Russian counterparts. They also addressed some Russian elite.

Therefore, the conversations about our release were ongoing on the sidelines. On the sixth day, one of those who transported us to the basement came and said that "respectable people" asked for us. I do not know who these "respectable people" are.

Yuriy and I were put in the car and taken to Chongar, where the dividing line was established. We were transferred into the hands of the MIA of Ukraine in exchange for some Russian officials. I do not know who exactly it was.

It was a pure crime. Thuggish paramilitary structure. I understand that it had been prepared long before the Russians attacked Crimea. I use the following image: when you go to the bottom, then you fear, and when you reach the bottom, it is not scary any more, since from the bottom you can see the dangers above. So, we were in the bottom. In the establishments, which we visited, the Russian Kubans and some other Russians felt like at home.

They were particularly opposed to the media, because the journalists could tell about the crimes committed during the annexation. It was particularly hard to work in Sevastopol, where I come from. There, you inevitably were questioned about who and what you were, unless you had a pass from Russian television. We managed to slip there somehow, but we were out of luck in Simferopol."

On May 14, 2014, Yaroslav Pilunskiy was denied entry to Russia. He was detained at Sheremetyevo airport and sent to Kyiv.

"I was invited for the video shooting in Moscow, says Pilunskiy. At Sheremetyevo airport, the passport control officer stopped me, and six hours later deported me with a certificate under unknown article 114 on the border crossing rules. The lawyers failed to find such an article. I did not apply to the Russian embassy. The Russian press published an article mentioning the deportation of the "coordinator of the neo-Nazi underground in Crimea" Yaroslav Pilunskyi."

Article 114 of the Criminal Code of RF reads as follows, "Infliction of a serious or moderate injury by exceeding the limits of required defense or in excess of the measures required to detain the perpetrator." It is in no way related to the border crossing.

"That is, since I appeared in the hands of a criminal group, as Pilunskyi commented on the incident to the reporters, the information about which is not available even to the Ministry of Defense of Russia, I became persona non grata for this country. Poor peaceful "thugs" suffered during the interrogation. It appears that I, with my hands tied and a towel around my head, resisted them. They were so demoralized, that they did not come any more, not having learned from us when the "Right Sector" will come to Crimea?

The effects for Russia were so serious that at Sheremetyevo airport I was kept exclusively indoors and was taken to the toilet with escort, and my passport was returned only in Kyiv," added Pilunskiy.

Sevastopol detective

The history of the departure of **Tetiana Rykhtun**, the director of Sevastopol media center IRS Sevastopol from Crimea, looks like a detective story. Initially, accompanied by a guard, she left the city under cover of night, and then left for Kyiv by the last train before the so-called "referendum". This decision was preceded by threats, attacks and search in the media center, which put an end to the work of the independent press center and editorial board of 911se-vastopol.org.

Tetiana Rykhtun, the director of Sevastopol media center IRS Sevastopol. After the occupation of Crimea moved to Kyiv. Photo from her archive.

"In early March 2014, I was shooting the blockade of the headquarters of the Naval Forces of Ukraine by the so-called "self-defense of Sevastopol," says Tetiana, *behind which the men in uniform were hiding. The scenario was itemized: angry protesters demanded the military personnel leave the city, because it poses a threat to civilians. And men with guns are silently standing behind these people. It was clear that they came here from somewhere to stand along the military unit perimeter.*

My attempt to find out where they came from ended very quickly with an attack. All I remember is a tall man, a blow at the head, I am lying on the ground and someone takes the camera out of my hands.

My requests to the so-called "people's mayor" of Sevastopol nominated by the Russians and Ukrainian police failed. We lost the camera with footage, which proved that regular military units of Russia stayed in the territory of Sevastopol and participated in blocking Ukrainian military units.

The doctor, whom I consulted that day, cared not so much about my health, as about whose side I took. Only next day I managed to find a doctor who examined me and diagnosed cerebral edema.

Our press center was established in 2009 in Sevastopol on the initiative of several Crimean journalists as access to media resources for NGOs and activists. I led this project from the beginning. We provided a free tribune to the city residents so that they could inform the authorities of painful questions in the life of Sevastopol. Therefore, the officials and MPs regularly heard criticism addressed to them on television.

When a year later another project, 911sevastopol.org, appeared, the journalists focused on officials and MPs, who worked not for the benefit of the city, but for their welfare. One of the most high-profile investigations was material on how the Donetsk environment of the President of Ukraine Viktor Yanukovych stole two hundred hectares of orchards and vineyards with the tacit consent of local authorities from the city in 2012.

During Yanukovych's ruling, it has became more difficult to work, but the authorities did not dare to close the resource, although there were repeated attempts to do the same. When during the Maidan, in January 2014, we wrote that, despite the dramatic events in Kyiv, the construction of a palace for Yanukovych is still ongoing on Cape Aya, on the Southern coast of Crimea, the pressure on my family, my business and my son started.

Despite the tyranny of the Party of Regions, which was then in power, it shunned struggling with journalists by force, shunned the publicity.

Since the beginning of the annexation, things changed for the worse. Once the Russians landed in Sevastopol, we started covering their activities, including telling the truth about blocking of Ukrainian military units. We were the only source of information in Sevastopol, which honestly told about the events at the military base.

As such, those who were eager for power did not like us. First, there was an attack on me at the walls of the headquarters of the MIA of Ukraine, followed by an attempt to intimidate me. A stranger began throwing stones at me for no apparent reason. It was clear that the press center and editors were under threat. My colleagues from Kyiv even brought armored jackets for journalists' safety.

A few days later, they became the basis for criminal prosecution due to illegal possession of special equipment. On March 13, at the end of the day, a dozen of people in camouflage, who introduced themselves as the "self-defense of Sevastopol", came to the office to investigate, as they said, "the scene."

Search in IRS Sevastopol media center. Picture from archive of Tetiana Rukhtun.

They called the police, who acted on their side. Within six hours, the police shook up everything in the press center and editorial board. Since the police failed to find four kilograms of explosives, as alleged by the "self-defense", they decided to charge us with another criminal offence.

Then we were able to ward off this charge with the help of a lawyer, human rights activists from the Ukrainian Parliament Commissioner Office for Human Rights and fellow journalists who quickly spread the news about the search.

After midnight, our colleagues began to call and suggested we leave the peninsula. I agreed, and the next day I, accompanied by a specialist of the international security agency, was taken to Simferopol.

For a day, I was hiding at a cottage near Simferopol, while the experts were addressing logistical issues, since the railway station and airport were under Russian control. However, on the eve of the "referendum" on March 15, "self-defense" and Russian Cossacks left the railway station. This allowed me, accompanied by a guard, to catch the last train to Kyiv."

Currently, Tetiana Rykhtun works in Kyiv as the chief editor of the information broadcast on the UA: Crimea TV channel, part of public broadcasting.

Kerch ferry service takeover

In Kerch, about 200 kilometers from Simferopol, another dramatic situation was developing, since there is the ferry between the Crimean Peninsula and the Krasnodar Territory of Russia. The distance between them is less than five kilometers.

Huge ferries, both automotive and rail, operate there. They allowed carrying both civilian and military transport. Therefore, it was of strategic importance.

On March 6, 2014, the journalist of Kerch FM website **Olena Lysenko** received information that the Russians carry a new batch of military equipment by ferry. She immediately got in the car with her colleague and went to the ferry service.

> "Some unknown people treat us, the inhabitants of this city, quite brazenly. The set their own orders, known only to them, and threaten to punish their violation."

"At the entrance, there were military trucks, says Lena, *and near the barrier, we saw armed men in military uniforms and masks. With no sign of recognition. In other words, these were Russian military personnel.*

The ferry service workers, Ukrainian border guards and customs officers were standing aside. It seemed that they had been removed from their duties.

There was a man in uniform, whom I met on the eve near Ukrainian military units. He was one of those who blocked the units. He clearly belonged to the commanders. He was approached by an elderly woman who was excited and said something about the border-recruits. She meant the Ukrainian military men. The man replied that only contractors work there. I filmed the dialogue with my camera. He made a gesture and said that I was not allowed to shoot here. I asked why. He waved at us and a crowd of Cossacks ran towards my colleague and me.

Men with whips in their hand, in boots and colored trousers rushed at us. It would look like a funny movie with elements of folklore, unless it was so scary.

For about four hundred meters, my colleague and I were blatantly pushed in the back. My colleague covered me. They told us offensive words, something like "you are nobody." Perhaps, because of the stress, I started answering them that I was born here, and my father was a Soviet officer.

They made sure that we got into our car. Because of excitement, my colleague failed to start the car. Then one of them returned. My colleague opened the car window, and he said, "Well, excuse us!" Apparently, something human awakened in them.

I think some Cossacks were not Cossacks at all, but the dressed up Russian intelligence officers. They spoke in Russian, pronouncing unstressed "o" as "a" in Russian words. Don or Kuban Cossacks do not speak like this. These are rather Muscovites or residents of the central part of the country. Perhaps, the army, not to lose the image of "polite people", dressed up the soldiers so that they could do the dirty work.

When I came to the editor's office it appeared that I forgot to turn off the camera, so all the chatter with our pursuers was recorded. Having listened to it, my colleagues were shocked. Some unknown people treat us, the inhabitants of this city, quite brazenly. The set their own orders, known only to them, and threatened to punish violators."

The ex-director of Arguments of the Week. Kerch, journalist **Olena Yurchenko** said that the ferry service was first used to transport people from Russia a few days before the incident was Olena Lysenko occurred, on February 27, 2014.

"Imagine if in Kyiv all trains suddenly stopped and no one explained what was going on, says Olena. This is what happened at the Kerch ferry service then. It was closed for ordinary citizens. It turned out that that night many people were transported by bus from Russia. Our reporters found

those buses. They were standing on the sidelines with the windows closed by curtains.

I managed to see that there were people in Cossacks' form and in uniform inside. They clearly did not want to communicate not only with the media, but also with anyone, and roughly dismissed the journalists' questions. They only said that they were pilgrims. Apparently, they were saying the same thing to the other journalists, because this information was disseminated in the press.

We did not believe that these were pilgrims. However, we did not understand then what kind of people they were or why they came here.

Olena Yurchenko, in 2014 a director of Arguments of the Week. Kerch (Argumenty niedelii.Kerch), after the occupatoon she woved to Kyiv.

The next day, it was reported that these people slept in the Orthodox Church of the Moscow Patriarchate in Komsomolsk Park. Kerch citizens made pictures from skyscrapers near the church showing the tents in the church courtyard. These were the first "green men" we saw.

Later, Larysa Shcherbula, the head of the administration appointed by the Russians published on her Facebook page the picture of the Russian soldiers praying inside the church. She wrote that the Russian authorities of Kerch were very grateful to the priest of the church for sheltering the Russian military in those early days. These pictures were made when Putin was saying that there is no Russian military there. So we can say that annexation began with Kerch."

Olena Yurchenko remembers that first the Russian soldiers who appeared at the ferry service did not speak to anyone. They were standing somewhere near the military car. They could be seen from afar. They behaved aggressively.

"However, they became more and more numerous every day, says Olena. *One day we came and saw two trucks. Next day, there were more trucks, and they were arranging the firing-point, right at the place at the Kerch ferry service were the tourist buses used to stop.*

We were making photos, video, releasing daily news. We hoped that someone sitting in Kyiv read and saw that the Russian military grouping was intensifying. We were hoping for a response, for protection.

On March 3, 2014, when we came to shoot, Russian soldiers approached us and said that we had to take the camera and go away. We tried to talk to them, to explain that we were on our own land, in our hometown, and not in the territory of the military unit.

They have pointed their weapons at us and behaved very aggressively. I saw a military man walking from the ferry to the firing-point, which they made of bags filled with sand. I was told that he was the chief.

I took a step forward to come up and talk to him. I thought maybe the soldiers did not understand. Maybe he would understand that we just did our job, and we had the right to be here.

However, he pulled his hand from afar in my direction in a rejecting gesture and said loudly, "We won't talk!" Soldiers did not let me go there. They pointed arms at us and prevented us from passing or continuing the shooting.

A Kerch police officer was standing at some distance. He looked at us and smiled. I have known this police officer for many years; he has always worked there. Apparently, there was an on-duty point. He, the Ukrainian police officer, was standing and smiling when the military men of a foreign country ran the show in our territory. I was very angry.

I went to the gate through which the cars came to the ferry and then to the ferryboat. There was a booth with a window in which the border guards were checking documents.

There were two of our officers and a Russian soldier inside. He was in black uniform. I start talking to them, "Are you all right?" They look at me and grinned as if I am a fool. "Yes – they say – we are ok. Why do you ask?" I said I saw that something wrong was going on there, since there was a soldier from a foreign country. I asked, "Did you see they have attacked us recently?" They say they have not seen. I say, "At least give me a hint. I'm going to the town now. I can tell something. Maybe, an armed seizure occurred?" They just laughed at me.

I said, "Can you explain to me what is happening?" They turned back, looked at the Russian and said, "Why don't you ask him." I asked. Certainly, he did not reply.

In general, the Russian soldiers rarely stoop to talking to us. They treated us as if we were not people. Then they put guards on the approaches to the ferry, and it has become impossible to go there."

Olena Lysenko shares that immediately after the seizure of the government buildings in Simferopol, they hoped that some secret service was about to come and free them. However, no such thing happened.

"When Kerch ferry was captured, she continues, we realized that some irreversible changes were occurring. There was something that could not be reversed. At least in the near future.

I still went to the military units blocked by the Russian invaders and said what was going on at our website. I was threatened frequently. They wrote me on Facebook, and sent letters by mail.

I used to engage in investigative journalism so I am accustomed to threats. However, now they were trying to implement them. Once we came to the garage and found that someone had tried to burn our Toyota, which our family bought a few months earlier. Attackers threw a rope saturated with fuel into the garage and set it on fire. Fortunately, it extinguished. Apparently, they decided not to proceed because the place was guarded."

The editor in chief of the Kerch. FM website, **Iryna Siedova** said that the pro-Russian activists' brutalities against journalists commenced yet before the Russian troops seized government buildings in Simferopol. She claims that Russian forces began rocking the situation in an organized manner at the beginning of the third week of February 2014, immediately after the President of Ukraine Viktor Yanukovych fled to Russia after shooting of dozens of people on the Maidan in Kyiv.

"On February 22, I was invited to speak as a journalist at a meeting of pro-Ukrainian forces, says Iryna. I went to the podium and said only two phrases, "I am Iryna Siedova. I am a journalist." And then an egg was thrown at me. I was approached by a big lad in hogging pants, looking like

a typical thug, one of those who attacked the protesters on Independence Square in Kyiv. Someone else came up. They pushed me away from the podium, and broke it.

Then the pack of these nobs knocked a man, who tried to calm the situation, to the ground. There were seven or more. That gang was beating the man by their feet until blood.

Several people and I were taken through the crowd in a police car. Later the journalists filmed videos when those who beat us were receiving money."

The director of the editorial office of Arguments of the Week. Kerch, journalist Olena Yurchenko filmed these events on video.

"This rally lowered the bar of morality, says Olena. *We used to see the mass actions. The Communists came, the workers who were not paid their salary protested. But the public beating of people has never happened. It was the first time. We saw the impotence of the police. We saw what a fine line separates civilized life from ruin.*

I was in the midst of an aggressive crowd. I was filming. And it was very scary, because aggressive people were from all sides, front, rear and laterally. I was filming, and the continuous feeling of insecurity was running high. I did not know what to expect, to be beaten or to get a knife tucked under the rib. These people were absolutely "frostbitten". It was very scary.

I saw that the action is well coordinated. There were men with radios giving commands."

Two days later, Iryna Siedova, the editor in chief of Kerch. FM, went to shoot the pro-Russian rally:

"I came there with a small video camera. But my face was shown in the news and on YouTube, where the video from that first meeting collated more than eight hundred thousand views. Two persons saw and recognized me, came up and dragged me somewhere behind the Lenin Monument, away from the public place. One can only guess what they would have done with me there.

However, I was not at loss. I recalled the advice from human rights activists on how to behave in such cases. I had screamed loudly, "Fire!

Fire!!" They were confused and released me. I ran to the police, and they took me away by their car.

After that, I did not dare to work at public events. It was risky, least of all to my health. I helped the foreign journalists and Ukrainians from Kyiv to shoot, and guided them.

I accompanied Al Jazeera TV channel to the ferry. Previously, they were beaten in Sevastopol. Their tires were punctured; they were attacked by Cossacks there. They saw Cossacks in midstream and said that would not go there and would shoot from behind the fence. I suggested them to approach from another side, where there is no troop, where they could make a good picture.

We were driving around the ferry, followed by a gray Zhiguli. I understand that we were tailed by graymen. We arrived at the place and started shooting. Suddenly, a man in sneakers with a radio gets out of that car and approaches us. He asks us, "Why are you shooting here?" They explain to him through an interpreter that they are foreign journalists willing to shoot the ferry. He chats to someone on the radio. Then he said, "Ok. Shoot."

They ask him, "Who are you?" He says, "Self-defense of Crimea". He has a clear pronunciation of unstressed "o" as "a" in Russian words, as it is spoken in Moscow. Our people do not pronounce the words like this. To put in differently, the Russian pretended to be the local.

Next time, in the first week of March, Kyiv journalists and I went to the ninth kilometer, to the Ukrainian military unit. There, around the unit, there were the armored vehicles dug into the ground. They replaced the trucks with soldiers of the Black Sea Fleet, who came here first. It was a kind of rotation.

My colleagues were shooting, and I got out of the car, too, to shoot the armored vehicle. Then a soldier comes up and says, "Take off your camera, for my optical sight sees farther than your camera." Then I realize that it makes no sense to show my journalistic license to such a personality."

On March 17, 2014, the day after the so-called "referendum" on the status of Crimea, Iryna moved to the mainland. She believes that she has no prospect under the new government.

"My husband worked in the marine business, she says, getting a good salary, good even according to European standards. His work has not been

associated with journalism in any way. He helped ships entering the Cri-
mean ports to execute documents. When I left, our daughter and he re-
mained there until summer, so that the child quietly completed her studies
at school.

My man didn't want to leave. But he wanted me to leave, because he
worried of my life and health, for I was shooting the occupation process
extensively, and accompanied foreign journalists. I received threats from
the Russian military, including on Facebook. So he did not object to my
leaving. I think he was hoping that I would stay on the mainland for a few
months and come back.

I have lived in Kyiv for some time and was convinced that my men
needs to leave Crimea, too, since the occupied territory is not a joke, and
his business will perish, just like journalism. It was quite a difficult pro-
cess. After all, when a man has worked all his life at a stable job, it is very
difficult for him to go to an unknown place, to a city where there is no ship
and no sea, while all his work over the past ten years has been connected
to the sea, to abandon stable life, apartment, relatives, and all friends. Nev-
ertheless, he made this strategic decision. When our daughter finished the
fourth grade, he took her and went to me. Since then, we have been living
in Kyiv.

At the time when Ukraine controlled Crimea, there were lots of prob-
lems with freedom of speech. Any inquiry in the deals of the then Kerch
major, Oleg Osadchy, resulted in persecution for our Kerch.FM website.
After the publication, an SBU agent came to us and asked about how we
got American grants. He said that maybe we were American spies, and
arranged interrogations.

Once, the journalists and I were not allowed to the city government,
where our colleague was detained on the first floor. We called the police.
And it opened a criminal case.... against us. The case was not based on
interference in journalists' activities by the city government guard, but it
was instituted against me and journalist Serhiy Mokrushyn for alleged
false call of the police.

Our radio station broadcast was blocked, the water supply was cut
off. This is how we worked. However, publicity could help stopping this
pressure. We could turn to the union of journalists, the Kyiv media to
support us. Local authorities were not holy, but the NGOs and public
opinion forming has let us stop the pressure on their part.

Thus, even under pressure, with nerves, but we were an independent media. No one dictated to us from above, nobody imposed strict editorial policy, and there was no censorship. We did not have our materials approved by anyone. We wrote what we thought. We were an independent media covering the whole Maidan, all the occupation process, and we were a law unto ourselves.

Now it's impossible. Kerch.FM website, which I created with my colleagues, removed a part of the materials to avoid the disgrace of the occupation authorities. You will not find there any criticism of power. Everything is "within reason" in terms of Russia.

Incidentally, the marine business turned down, as I predicted. The former fellow of my husband does not have a sweet life anymore."

After moving to Kyiv, Iryna Siedova started working at Hromadske Radio, where she has worked for several years. Now she works in the Crimean Human Rights Group NGO.

On April 1, 2015, Olena Yurchenko retired from the editor's office Agrumenty Nedeli. Kerch [ENG: Arguments of the Week. Kerch—ed.]. She did not intend to remain in the profession, since she realized that under the new government it is impossible to work as a full-fledged journalist:

"For some time, I was preparing the materials for Ukraina channel. Then Radio Svoboda contacted me, and I started working for them. The cooperation lasted until mid-June.

Then I called the chief editor of Radio Svoboda's project Krym. Realii [ENG: Crimea. Realities—ed.]. I said that we couldn't stay here. I was afraid that I wouldn't find job in Kyiv. I have no relative on the mainland, so it was very scary to leave everything we had and go to nowhere with a child. However, I was offered the position of editor of the Krym. Realii."

Olena Lysenko could not leave immediately because of personal circumstances. She moved to Kyiv in the summer of 2015. Olena works with the Crimean Human Rights Group.

"I have lived under Russian rule for a year and saw firsthand all the charms of a police state, says Lysenko. *You cannot breathe here almost*

physically. Whatever problems are on the mainland doesn't matter, it is the area of freedom."

Injured journalist's camera

When Russian troops were invading the administrative part of the Belbek airfield in Crimea, in the northwestern part of Sevastopol, they injured a journalist, and not only failed to help him, but also took away his camera. This episode was filmed by the Associated Press reporter, **Adam Pemble**. It was posted on Youtube on March 22, 2014. The episode I mean starts with the 18th second.

"Three hours before the assault, says **Valeriy Kulyk**, the Ukrainian fixer of the American journalist, *the wedding party was celebrated at Belbek. The officer, I guess the lieutenant, got married.*

They knew that the assault will occur, and it will be impossible to meet guests after it. So they were in a hurry. At that time, in Crimea, despite all the problems, not all the soldiers believed that the Russians were the enemy, imagine the situation like when the masters are fighting, the slaves have their bangs cracking. Only after the war in Donbas, the Russians have consciously become enemies. That is why the approach was careless.

They laid the tables on the parade ground. It was a small celebration. Then, at about three to four o'clock an assault began.

First the Cossacks were running around, fussing, but did not climb the fence. After a while, an armored vehicle went down the hill. Russian soldiers exited it. The armored vehicle rammed the fence. They ran inside, threw light and noise grenades and shot upwards.

At that time, two photojournalists were near the fence. When the fence collapsed, one of them was pressed by a piece of cement. An armed men in camouflage uniform approached him and took away his camera, having kicked him. Instead of helping him, he moved on. I do not know who these journalists were. Some Western publication.

Then the Russians gathered all journalists and searched them one by one. They seized all the memory cards. When we were searched, one of the military men said, "Well, so you came here to tell lies about us, to say that we all are bad?"

We managed to hide two memory cards behind the body armor, containing video of seizing the camera. We had two cards then. The first contained the wedding, and the second – the time of assault. We left the wedding card in the camera just in case the soldiers tried removing the cards, so that they seized the less important one."

The takeover occurred on March 22, 2014, after the so-called "referendum" on the status of the Crimea. It was one of the last takeovers of the Ukrainian military facilities in in Crimea.

However, the injured journalist talked about it on Facebook. It was a photo correspondent from Russian city St. Petersburg, **Aleksandr Aksakov**.

"The Reuters photographer was next to me. We were filming the SWAT entrance to the base. Then I heard the cry of this photographer, and mechanically ran (I do not understand where) and felt something very heavy hitting my head, wrote Aleksandr Aksakov. Then I remember trying not to lose consciousness. I fell to the ground and felt that my leg is squeezed. When a few moments later I was able to think of what had happened, I saw the armored vehicle moving at me.

A flashback: my right foot is squeezed by a concrete fence, ten inches from my feet, just on the fence, an armored vehicle is standing. My foot and a part of the ankle were squeezed. I tried to pull my leg out (with or without a boot...). I failed. Then the Reuters photographer (THANK YOU, MAN!) stood in front of the armored vehicle and began shouting that the journalist was injured. The armored vehicle stood for a moment and moved back a bit."

As witnesses to the incident later told[6] to Telekrytyka, the journalist was helped by Reuters reporter, **Baz Ratner** (Israel).

The Russians once again demonstrated that they prevent journalists from covering the situation objectively. Past events have shown that they are fighting the media systemically in a variety of ways, i.e. by restricting access to information, intimidation and arrest of journalists, brutal beating of people with press cards, not allowing international observers to work, and using other means. The

---

6   In Belbek, the Reuters photographer, rescuing a Russian colleague, stopped the armored vehicle / Telekrytyka, 23.03.2014. URL: http://ru.telekritika.ua/pravo/2014-03-23/91841

future events, after the illegal annexation, have shown that they are not going to abandon this policy.

After the expansion of the aggression against Ukraine on February 24, 2022, Russia seized the city of Berdyansk in Zaporizhzhia region, where Stanislav Selivanov had lived before the war in 2014 began. On April 21 the so-called military commandant of the city of Berdyansk — Russian colonel Artyom Bardin — released a decree regarding the appointment of deputies to the so-called city mayor. Among them was Selivanov, who was supposed to be responsible for social matters.

Later, on September 6, Bardin's car was blown up by Ukrainian partisans. He died in hospital from the injuries received.

The city of Berdyansk is situated on the shore of the Sea of Azov, 200 kilometers from the regional center Zaporizhzhia. This city was highly important for Ukrainian trade since there was a functioning seaport, through which significant volumes of metallurgical and agricultural products were transported.

Besides that, it was a popular resort with a 20 km shoreline with beaches. Right now, they are deserted.

On May 25, the website "Primorka.city", which was not under the control of the occupants, said the summer season was being disrupted. Since vacationers were the main source of income for the majority of Berdyansk citizens, the disruption of the season led to the impoverishment of the inhabitants.

On September 7, 2022, The SBU declared six suspected collaborators, among which Selivanov was listed:

"Another collaborator — Stanislav Selivanov is one of the founders of 'Putin's Political Party' in Ukraine and he has been actively cooperating with enemy since 2014. The resident of the city of Berdyansk took active part in the annexation of the Crimean Peninsula and was awarded with a medal 'for the returning of Crimea'. Later he held a position of a member of the 'Council of DPR'. After the occupation of the part of Zaporizhzhia region, he was 'promoted' and appointed 'deputy mayor of Berdyansk on social matters.'"

Just like other suspected traitors, he will face up to 15 years in prison.

Deprived of the Right to a Profession

Chornomorka was the first to shut down

On February 28, 2014, the author of these lines visited the editor's office of Arguments of the Week. Crimea, located in the capital city of Crimea, Simferopol. It was growing dark, but on that day and on the day before, the events that will change the fate of the country and even the world were taking place, so no one was leaving.

After five o'clock it was reported that armed men came to the Crimean state TV station (KDTRK). The journalists perceived it as a logical continuation of what happened yesterday.

Since the seizure of government buildings, the editor's office of Arguments of the Week. Crimea had been working non-stop.

Stanislav Yurchenko. Photo by Krym (RFE/RL).

"Control of the tower meant control of the Crimean air. Controlling the tower, one could decide who would broadcast there, and who won't."

"We had a lot of friends, colleagues, who worked in state TV, recalls the photo and video correspondent of the newspaper, Stas Yurchenko, who now works in the Radio Liberty project Krym. Realii. *I do not remember exactly who, but we were called and told that soldiers seized the state TV. Not only was the TV company important, but also the broadcasting tower located in its territory. Control of the tower meant control of the Crimean air. Controlling the tower, one could decide who would broadcast there, and who won't. We were well aware of the implications of this step. So we quickly got together and went to the scene."*

In the car were Alim Veliyev, the driver and videographer Stas Yurchenko, the photographer, and the author of these lines.

We arrived at KDTRK on Studentska Street when it was already dark. The company had a few buildings surrounded by a fence. One could only get in through the checkpoint. There were several police cars near the checkpoint gate.

No extraordinary movement was seen from the outside. We were approached by a woman around 50 who started screaming something like *"All sorts of journalists are walking here, showing lies, interfering with the life of ordinary people."*

At the checkpoint, we introduced ourselves and asked if we could pass. The guard refused.

We stood for some more time in front of the checkpoint, from where a group of people in police uniform came. To our question, they replied that there indeed are people in uniform, but they behave politely and no incident occurred. They got into their cars and left.

"I was shocked, says Stas Yurchenko today. *The soldiers came to the state structure, it must have been an extraordinary event! The police behaved as if nothing had happened, as if such things happen every day. No excitement. In the process of annexation and afterwards I found out that a huge part of security forces in Crimea and soldiers betrayed their oath. Therefore, from the distance of time, it is not surprising that they behaved this way. But then I was overwhelmed."*

We decided to return to the editor's office. From there, we called the head of KDTRK, Stepan Gulevatyi. He told us by telephone that there are two dozen armed men in the territory of his organization, who came to "protect the employees from eventual provocations."

Gulevatyi reported that they were from the Black Sea Fleet. *"I asked whether they were from Russia or Ukraine, but they did not respond,"* he added. Stepan Gulevatyi remained in the occupied Crimea after the annexation, but he resigned as KDTRK director, having switched to the state structures.

"Armed men, intelligent, without identification marks, talked to the director, we are safe, we are working," wrote Crimean journalist Tetiana Shamanayeva, who worked in KDTRK, on her Facebook page. Then she was quoted by[7] Arguments of the Week. Crimea.

Shamanayeva also reported that she personally saw three such persons, and that the speaker of the Crimean parliament Volodymyr Konstantinov came to talk them.

Now Tetiana Shamanayeva continues to work at the same channel, which after the occupation is called First Crimean.

Myroslav Mamchak, who has been the editor in chief of the broadcasting company of the Ministry of Defense of Ukraine Breeze for 16 years, says that the next day after the tower seizure KDTRK released a fake news story that a key ship of the Ukrainian navy, frigate "Hetman Sahaidachnyi" raised the Russian flag.

"Before that Stepan Gulevatyi, the head of KDTRK, called me, says Myroslav Mamchak, *with regard to this fact. I contacted the ship, which at that time was in the port of Souda in Crete. I clarified the situation, called Gulevatyi and said that was not true. However, the channel released this fake news on air. Gulevatyi immediately began to serve the invaders, spreading the news intended to mislead the Ukrainian military and civilians."*

After a while, the journalists of the Information Office of the Crimean Tatar programs at KDTRK said they disagreed with the

---

7   Lawlessness in Crimea: a TV center and a radio center is seized in Simferopol / Donbass.ua, 28.02.2014. URL: http://donbass.ua/news/ukraine/2014/02/28/ bespredel-v-krymu-v-simferopole-zahvachen-telecentr-i-radiocentr.html

current policy of the broadcaster and would not be aired until the "referendum." It was reported on Facebook by journalist **Shevket Ganiyev**.

The deputies of the Crimean Parliament, which was controlled by the Russians at that time, transferred the Krym State Television and Radio Company and the Center of Radio Transmission of the ARC State Enterprise to the subordination of the Autonomous Republic. The resolution was passed on March 11, 2014 at an extraordinary meeting of the Crimean Parliament, held without the press.

By order of the State Committee for TV and Radio Broadcasting of Ukraine dated March 12, Stepan Gulevatyi was dismissed from his post of the head of the Krym STRC. The broadcaster explained[8] that this is a gross violation of the law on Television and Radio, a violation of the charter of the state broadcaster, and default under the state order. The Television and Radio Company did not provide any detail. However, de facto it is clear that Gulevatyi transferred the broadcaster to serve the occupiers.

Two days after KDTRK and tower seizure, on March 3, 2014, the deputies of the Crimean Parliament threatened to block the work of the media allegedly distorting the real situation in Crimea.

The statement of the Crimean Parliament, which at that time was under Russian control, noted that *"many media circulated in Ukraine found themselves trapped in an information war aimed at achieving two goals, to create panic among the population and to impose misconceptions about the situation in social and political life of the republic on the residents of Ukraine."*

Crimean authorities expressed confidence that the events occurring in Crimea were covered one-sidedly. *"The television programs, talk shows and news stories did not present the views of the Crimeans and Crimean authorities. The word is available only to supporters of the so-called "Maidan" having no real support among the Crimean population. Deliberately false information was provided to create the illusion of military intervention, to give the audience the confidence that the peaceful life of the Crimeans is threatened,"* read the statement.

---

8   State Committee dismissed the heads of Krym STRC and Sevastopol RDTRK/Telekrytyka, 11.03.2014. URL: http://ru.telekritika.ua/rinok/2014-03-11/91352

In this regard, the Crimean authorities said *„unless the negative information campaign stops, they will be forced to cut off the flow of false and biased information to protect the population from its negative effects."*

On the same day, March 3, private the Black Sea broadcasting company, popularly called Chornomorka was off the air.

> "Russian occupiers used the media as a weapon; they distorted information and forced the audience to believe in their lie."

"The subsequent script was clear, says the founder and the co-owner of „Chornomorka", **Andriy Senchenko,** now the head of the Power of Law NGO, who at that time worked as a deputy head of the Administration of the Acting President of Ukraine. *When they took control of the Parliament and government buildings, everything else was just a trick. Clearly, there was no resistance, against both Konstantinov* (Volodymyr Konstantinov, the head of the Verkhovna Rada of Crimea — ed.) *and Aksionov* (Serhiy Aksionov, the head of government appointed during the occupation of Crimea — ed.) *took this for granted. It's not something that someone takes over, and the government resists. No, they were invaders from one side of the barricades."*

Black Sea Broadcasting Company was founded in 1993. It included Assol radio. After the annexation of Crimea, the editor's office had to move to Kyiv.

The founder and co-owner of the broadcaster was entrepreneur and politician Andriy Senchenko, who was elected to the Ukrainian parliament as a member of Batkivshchyna All-Ukrainian Union headed by Yulia Tymoshenko. At the time of the Crimea occupation, he was the acting deputy head of the Presidential Administration of Ukraine. Now he is the head of the Power of Law NGO. He believes that the Russian invaders turn Crimea into a military base.

"As for Chornomorka, continues Senchenko, practically at the beginning of March, the invaders cut off its broadcast, and on these frequencies they illegally launched Russia 24 TV channel. Given that from nineteen transmitters through which the Black Sea TV and Radio Company was broadcasting in Crimea, only six were owned by the Radio Broadcasting Television Center of Ukraine (RBTC), Ukrainian enterprises, and thirteen

transmitters were the property of Chornomorka. All this was captured, Chornomorka was disabled and replaced by "Russia 24"."

When asked why Chornomorka was the first to shut down, Senchenko explains:

"Chornomorka was 20 years old then. This is the broadcaster, which raised a whole generation of Crimeans, the most popular local television station. He was patriotic, pro-Ukrainian, and did not broadcast Russian propaganda slogans.

The rest was bought by some pro-Russian structures and was controlled by Moscow, or became like the Crimean State Broadcasting Company, allegedly a mouthpiece of the state, but releasing anti-state news on air. In fact, "Chornomorka", Assol radio, weekly Sobytiya and ATR channel remained on the side of Ukraine. On the other side, there are all Russian channels broadcasted in cable networks, and, of course, channels such as Inter, which served information in a fairly specific manner, playing up to Russian propaganda."

So, on March 3, 2014, three days after seizure of KDTRK and transmitting tower, Chornomorka air was shut down. On March 9, Crimea cut off the analog broadcasting of all Ukrainian channels. However, they continued to work in cable networks.

The then reporter of ATR channel **Ibraim Umerov** witnessed Russians resetting the transmitting equipment on the tower.

"That day KDTRK held a press conference, but I don't remember what it was dedicated to, says Ibraim. *We were not accredited, but we talked the guard's head off at the entrance and said that someone will meet us. We actually met colleagues from the Crimean Tatar editor's office.*

In the back yard, we saw green men, that is Russian military men. We also saw some unknown people reconfiguring equipment at the television tower. We showed it live. Seeing us, they were hiding, went inside the room, and then came back out and continued to work.

Surprisingly, we were not expelled. On that day, they quietly finished work. After that, the Ukrainian channels could not be watched on the peninsula."

"Instead of Inter TV channel, Crimea now broadcasts NTV, reported Interfax-Ukraine then, *instead of 1+1 – the first channel, instead of Ukrainian First National – Russia 1, instead of STB – Zvezda channel, instead of Channel 5 – TNT, instead of ICTV – Tatarstan-based TNV-Planet. The place of Chornomorka channel in the Crimean air was taken over by Russia 24. Instead of it, it is planned to launch a new channel Krym 24 soon. K1, TET, Mega, M1, New Channel, NTN, Ukraina and 2+2 are disabled, too. They are only available on cable networks."*

Meanwhile, the "Deputy Prime Minister" of the so-called "Crimean government", Olga Kovitidi denied the disabling of the Ukrainian television, *"On Sunday, some difficulties with Ukrainian channels broadcasting occurred in Simferopol due to technical reasons,"* she said to Interfax-Ukraine.

"We know about the problem; according to preliminary information, it is caused by technical failures. Nobody disabled the channels," added Kovitidi.

"Now I am in Sevastopol. Here all Ukrainian TV channels are work-ing properly, she said in a telephone conversation with the reporter. *It will take some time to determine the cause. We will find out what the failures are due to, and the broadcasting will be resumed."*

"Their actions were quite logical, comments on the Chornomorka co-owner Andriy Senchenko. *Russian occupiers used the media as a weapon; they distorted information and forced the audience to believe in their lie that a "junta from Kyiv" is coming to conquer them. The true coverage would prevent them from implementing their goals related to the Crimea annexation. So they disabled Ukrainian TV channels and re-stricted the other journalists' access to the scene in various ways."*

Working without equipment

On March 1, 2014, the day after the seizure of the Crimean State TV and Radio Company, the Center for Investigative Reporting known in Crimea and beyond was seized, too.

It was founded in 2008 in Simferopol. It had offices in six cities of Crimea. The Center was not only the media, but also the media platform hosting discussions of important social and political issues.

The leader of the Center is journalist **Valentyna Samar**, who was awarded by the Norwegian Fritt Ord Foundation and German ZEIT Foundation for her contribution to journalism in Eastern Europe.

The editor in chief of the Center, Valentyna Samar recalls that they learned that they were going to be captured from TV streams. They managed to lock themselves in the studio. Meanwhile, near the captured House of Trade Unions in Simferopol, the people with St. George's Ribbons beat the cameraman of the Crimean Tatar ATR channel **Rustem Murtazayev**, who led the live broadcast of the capture. The traffic police officers who were standing nearby did not respond to it. When the TV channel guard came, the journalist and the cameraman were released.

Valentyna Samar, the leader of the Center for Investigative Reporting in Simferopol. After the occupation moved to Kyiv. Photo from krymr.org (RFE/RL)

"On March 1, the first non-governmental organization, our Center for Investigative Reporting, was captured, says Valentyna Samar. We leased a room in the House of Trade Unions, facing the central Lenin

Square, the captured Government of Crimea. We usually gathered many journalists; this place was well-known.

Unmarked people come to us. After them, came the then leaders of the marginal pro-Russian organizations, Kostiantyn Knyryk and Serhiy Veselovskiy.

Knyryk was the then coordinator of the Eurasian Youth Union in Crimea, the organization, created with contribution of ideologue of the modern Russian chauvinism, the so-called "Russia's space" Aleksandr Dugin, who wants to revive the Russian empire. Knyryk also raved the empire, and openly spoke about it. He said that the main task of the organization is detach Crimea from Ukraine, and looked like a clown. The rallies of his organization were attended by no more than fifty people.

Veselovskiy was another parasite in the alleged field of the "fight against fascism" in Ukraine. He joined the Pavlo Sudoplatov Crimean Antifascist Movement. This organization originated in 2011, armed with naphthalene-soaked slogans of Soviet propaganda. Then, the organization intensified its activities in February 2014, shortly before the annexation.

They would have remained figures with meager popularity. But the Russian occupiers were in need of such people. The process of the peninsula annexation gave them weight and inflated those bubbles. Currently, Veselovskyi leads some crazy chauvinist propaganda program on the channel of the Russian-formed so-called "Donetsk People's Republic." And Knyryk acts as a political scientist and commentator, voicing the thesis from the Russian TV.

> "We work for the money of the Americans, as they said, for the money of the State Department. They do not like it. So they will pay money to us, and they will feed us if we work "properly"."

We have learned that they are going to capture us from the TV, from streams led by ATR journalists. We locked ourselves in the studio.

They were bursting at the House of Trade Unions, they were not let in, they broke the window and an old lady, who served as a concierge, had to open the door. They took the keys and opened the media center, but they didn't have the key to the room where we had locked ourselves in.

We watched their press conference given in our hall live. They said that they respected our professional work, but we had to work "properly." Now we work for the money of the Americans, as they said, for the money of the State Department. They do not like it. So they will pay money to us, and they will feed us if we work "properly".

They left, and we spent some more time in the editor's office. We still did not know who worked it, and they did not push us out right away. Most likely, it was synergy, since the deputy editor of the weekly Dzerkalo Tyzhnia [ENG: Mirror of the Week — ed.] *Yulia Mostova, with whose newspaper we cooperated, phoned everyone whom she could reach, the MP, the ex-dissident Mustafa Dzhemilev went to the head of the SBU Valentyn Nalyvaychenko, and people from Alfa special unit called me saying that they were going to unlock us. In short, after they left, we worked at this place for some time. On May 10 or 11, on the second floor of the House of Trade Unions, under our rooms, the so-called "self-defense of Crimea" settled. There they lived, ate and exercised.*

On May 14, 2014, the chief of staff of the self-defense of Crimea, Dmytro Prostakov, and five armed men entered my office without permission. I am not a person who can be frightened easily, but one can assume anything in this situation.

Two of them, crying "It is an underground studio. Call the FSB!" pushed our colleague, Vladlen Melnikov, out of the studio and blocked her entrance. Prostakov requested that I produce the documents on the room lease, on the right of the studio and agency to work, asked about the sources of funding and permission to work in Russia. I said that I would not talk to him until the armed men leave my office.

He reluctantly instructed them to leave, and they went out.

Then I called the Crimean parliament deputy Volodymyr Klichnykov, who was the then Chairman of the Federation of Independent Trade Unions of Crimea, appointed by the occupation authority, which owned this room. Klichnykov asked me to pass on the receiver to Prostakov. They talked, and then the latter left the room with his armed men.

> "We have been doing our job honestly. As professionally as we did it before. Much of what we were filming and writing then is now evidence to the court, including the International Criminal Court."

A few weeks later, the lessor's representatives informally asked the Center for Investigative Reporting to leave the House of Trade Unions, since it would be safer for all. We had to move to our partner organization, Chornomorska broadcasting company.

This is how we had worked until August 1. Many people looked at us like at suicides, some German channels shot a movie about us.

We called the occupiers the occupiers. We called the annexation the annexation. We called the illegal government the illegal government.

We have been doing our job honestly. As professionally as we did it before. Much of what we were filming and writing then is now evidence to the court, including the International Criminal Court.

This is true for various aspects, including the treason of the Chairman of the Appellate Court, who actually passed the entire judicial system to the invaders. This is the investigation of disappearances. Murders.

Our investigations were broadcasted by national channels, such as the murder of Reshat Ametov (found dead on March 15, 2014 after he participated in a peaceful protest against the Russian occupation of Crimea — author's note), *the disappearance of Tymur Shaimardanov* (he was active in protests against the occupation of Crimea — author's note). *We made videos about the missing people, explaining who they are, and all this was broadcasted on air by Chornomorka.*

Sometimes we were asked why they had been tolerating us for so long. Perhaps this is due to the fact that we were quite renowned. In April 2014, I spoke at the UN Security Council, presenting the findings on the monitoring of violations of the freedom of speech, freedom of opinion, and peaceful assembly. Our monitoring findings were included in the report of OSCE by the office of Dunja Mijatovic, the then Ombudsman for the Freedom of Speech in that organization. We also had extensive contacts with the Western media.

After our office was captured on March 1, we decided to be more public and declared that our room from now on is an international media center. We helped foreign journalists find interpreters, fixers, and were searching for the proper contacts for them. Our people were doing that intentionally.

We have become even more public than before. Perhaps this hampered the occupiers to do away with us openly.

Chornomorka was restricted continuously; their transmitters were captured in the early days of the annexation. Later on, the cable cameramen were prohibited to broadcast from them. This affected us, too, since we cooperated with it. The Internet and satellite remained. At that time, our Kyiv studio started broadcasting."

The reporter of the Center for Investigative Reporting Natalia Ko-korina recalls that the normal work stopped when the bailiffs slammed the equipment of Chornomorka and their Center:

"We were working normally until our accreditation to the Parliament and the Council of Ministers of Crimea was cancelled, after they were renamed by the occupying authority. We were told that they have become different, now Russian authorities. However, ATR was streaming continuously, and there were other accredited journalists, from which we could get some information and work.

Most of our colleagues turned away from us, and stopped communicating with us. They didn't even say hello to us. We became enemies to them, for we were holding to the pro-Ukrainian position and stressed that this takeover is illegal, it is annexation.

We moved to Chornomorka in July. We leased the room of the old studio. We arranged the editor's office and hanged a Ukrainian flag. And on August 1, the bailiffs rushed into the studio. First, we did not realize who it was.

Four stout men in civilian clothes suddenly broke into our studio and said, "Go away! You all!" We were three or four in the editor's office at that time. We ask, "Why do we have to go out. Who are you?" They gave no explanation, did not introduce themselves, just said "Get out!"

We tried to argue, to find out who they were. But they were forcing us to leave, so we had to pick up our personal belongings and go outside.

Standing on the street, we learned from the director of Chornomorka Liudmyla Zhuravliova that these are bailiffs. They came to seize the property by court order in the case of the Radio and TV Transmission Center (RTVTC) against the broadcaster. The case was allegedly related to the debt of Chornomorka. Finally, the broadcaster succeeded in court and the equipment was returned to Chornomorka and the Center for Investigative Reporting. But not everything was returned and not everything was in good working order."

"They brought a judgment, says the co-owner of Chornomorka An-driy Senchenko, which has not become final and binding yet. The appeal proceedings were not finished. After the invaders took control of the Radio and TV Transmission Center, they invented that Chornomorka allegedly owes an amount equivalent to about a thousand dollars to the enterprise for broadcasting. The ex-Ukrainian courts continued grinding out the

judgments, and there was a period when the judge signed the judgment in the name of the Russian Federation, but affixed a seal bearing the Ukrainian trident. It was they who grinded out the judgment far from the truth."

> "They carried all computers and television equipment outside and then threw it into the truck. They did not pile it up, but literally threw. Nobody cared whether it broke or not."

In front of the Verkhovna Rada (the parliament) of Crimea. Photo by Stanislav Yurchenko (RFE/RL)

"The bailiffs spread about the floors, continues Natalia Kokorina. *There were the other employees of Chornomorka. They also went out and we were standing outside as a crowd, while the bailiffs were taking stock of the property and seized it. We were not let in. Only the director, Zhuravliova, could pass. Certainly, she could not trace all property. The bailiffs seized the personal appliances of the company employees, too. Someone failed to take his personal bag, and after the invasion found that the money and flash cards were missing...*

It was like a sur. They carried all computers and television equipment outside and then threw it into the truck. They did not pile it up, but literally threw. Nobody cared whether it broke or not.

The assets of the Center for Investigative Reporting were taken away, too. We tried to explain to the head of this group that we were not

Chornomorka, and they had no right to take away our equipment, because we had nothing to do with debts and just leased the room. But it did not worry them. The director said, "We take it, and it's up to you to sort it out."

They threw our equipment into the trucks with the then broad-caster's equipment. No legal mechanism or standard was in force there."

"We certainly tried to put international pressure on Russia, says Andriy Senchenko. *In the summer of 2014, we approached the embas-sies. But at the same time, on August 23, a massive Russian invasion of regular troops from Russia to our territory began, and the Ilovaisk pocket occurred. On August 29, there was a massacre, when during the breakout from Ilovaisk, according to our investigation commission, up to a thousand Ukrainian soldiers were killed. Against this background, the mayhem in the broadcaster's premises in Crimea was a tiny thing, actually."*

> "Ultimately, the editor in chief Valentyna Samar decided to transfer the ed-itor's office to Kyiv, because we won't be allowed to work in Crimea."

Because of the threats and pressure, the editor's office was forced to move to Kyiv.

"When the equipment was taken away, a bus with the so-called "self-de-fense" arrived, continues Natalia Kokorina. *"Self-defense" sat in the smoking rooms. They were sitting there all night. I do not know whether they could go inside or slept outdoors, but they were there. We were not allowed into Chornomorka for several days, because the building was al-legedly attached.*

Then they cleared the building, and we were able to enter the terri-tory. It was all clogged by tins, cups, bags, remnants of food.

However, we did not have anything to work at. The broadcasts be-came impossible, but we were using our private laptops, trying to write something.

Ultimately, the editor in chief Valentyna Samar decided to transfer the editor's office to Kyiv. She asked me and everyone whether we were ready, whether we wanted it.

At that moment, I felt that I should better stay in Crimea. It was better for my conscience, because I thought that if everyone left Crimea, then who would defend it here? Someone had to stay.

I understood that she as the editor in chief could not stay, because this is the editor's office, the media, which must be preserved, which should work.

They left, and I stayed. For some time I continued working as a journalist at the Center for Investigative Reporting in Crimea. I was worked from home, until we were returned the equipment of Chornomorka and the Center for Investigative Reporting in December."

"Because Chornomorka was located on the occupied territory, says Andriy Senchenko, *it had no another defense mechanism available. It challenged the judgment and succeeded. Since the judgment of the trial court was absurd, for no debt existed, the appellate court had nothing to stick to. Based on the judgment, Chornomorka's equipment was returned."*

"I went to pick up the equipment, says Natalia Kokorina, *together with Chornomorka employees. It was stored in the warehouses of the radio and TV transmitting center. The equipment was in terrible condition, because it was stored in some half raw premises. We were missing computers, not to mention the flash cards or card readers.*

We could not understand what to do with it. Of course, we realized that all this equipment, which was handled by the Russian Federal Security Service, could be infected. We did not know whom we could entrust to check it.

It took us much time to make out where is Chornomorka's hardware and where is ours. When we started turning on the computers, I saw that the case of my computer contains the hard drive from Valentyna Samar's computer. It became clear that they not only turned on the computers, but also removed the hard drives, handed them over to their IT experts, and they downloaded all the information. Then they installed the hard drives back.

We moved the portion which could be transported to the mainland — cameras, computers. We took only one or two computers, because their hard drives contained very important information."

Now Chornomorka and the Center for Investigative Reporting moved to Kyiv and continue to cooperate. The editor in chief of the Center for Investigative Reporting Valentyna Samar leads a program at Chornomorka, in which she analyzes the current events related to Crimea.

"It was very difficult, tells Andriy Senchenko. For example, all my property, which I listed in good faith in my parliamentary return, was declared the property of the so-called "Republic of Crimea". I had nine years of business biography in Crimea. It was between work in the Crimean government, which I left in 1997, until I was elected the MP of Ukraine in 2006. I was in business for nine years, and it allowed me to support Chornomorka, to invest in it. Clearly, all these sources of funding remaining in Crimea. Therefore, in Kyiv, the studio had to be rebuilt all together. In fact, everything was done at the Kyiv bureau of Chornomorka at 2 Bankova Street, in a wing in the courtyard of the Writers Union. I had to collect the crumbs of the equipment and staff, but we resumed broadcasting."

"Freedom" does not fit here

In early December 2014, a fuss occurred at the Russian border checkpoint in Crimea. The border guard ran after the car, which entered neutral territory. He waved his hands requesting it to stop, and then aimed his gun at the car, but did not fire.

However, the driver did not stop. Contrarily, he stepped on the gas. He passed by a long queue to the Ukrainian checkpoint, got out of the car, showed his certificate to the border guards, said that he was a journalist and he had to pass as soon as possible to convey urgent and important material from Crimea to the editor's office. He was allowed to go.

Volodymyr Prytula. Photo by Krym (RFE/RL). Editor in chief of the Radio Liberty project Krym.

"Only in the Ukrainian territory I sighed with relief, recalls the editor in chief of the Radio Liberty project Krym. Realii **Volodymyr Prytula**. *When I passed the Russian border guards, they gave me a coupon to leave, but asked me to wait in the yard, because they wanted me to meet with the FSB. I realized that it was suspicious. I was waiting, as it seemed to me then, for quite a long time, and then came to the border guards, showed my coupon and said that I did not understand what to do. He asked me whether I had a stamp on my coupon. The stamp was available. "Well, so go," he said. I got into the car and drove quietly. Then, probably, someone noticed that I was leaving the checkpoint, the Russians came around and ordered to stop me. But it was too late."*

> "Since January 2014, I noticed someone watching me. I do not know who it was. Around the corner of the house, neighboring to mine, at Budionnogo Street, a van with tinted windows had been standing continuously. I noticed it. I was afraid that it could be paranoia."

It was the last visit of Volodymyr Prytula to Crimea. The editor's office of the Krym. Realii was evacuated from the peninsula annexed by Russia. The editors went to the mainland first, followed by a part of the "burned" journalists, on which the Russian special services began to press.

The idea to create a special Crimean media project on Radio Liberty came after the "referendum" on the status of Crimea. At that time there was a hope that, despite all the difficulties, it will continue to exist in Simferopol with the editor's office. The editor in chief of the Krym. Realii was a long-standing reporter of Radio Liberty in Crimea, Volodymyr Prytula.

"It was a risky decision, says Prytula, because we experienced a variety of brutal attacks in the course of the annexation.

Since January 2014, I noticed someone watching me. I do not know who it was. Around the corner of the house, neighboring to mine, at Budionnogo Street, a van with tinted windows has been standing continuously. I noticed it. I was afraid that it could be paranoia, but on February 27, when the Russians captured the administrative building in Simferopol, the minibus disappeared.

Besides this, I received outright threats. In particular, one of the former pro-Russian vice-prime ministers wrote to me on Facebook, saying, "do not worry, you'll get to Siberia. Russia will come here, and then you will find yourself in the Kolyma camps."

One of the most active pro-Russian activists said during the campaigns I was covering that my family and I would have troubles. Also, the people from the so-called "self-defense", having recognized me, approached and said, well, "Prytula, we know you, hold on. Haven't you sent your family away yet?"

Therefore, on March 1, I sent my wife and children away to relatives in Dnipropetrovsk region, and returned to work.

There were many cases of attacks on journalists. When my colleagues or I came to the pro-Russian events, I always faced the aggressive attitude of the crowd. For example, they tried to knock out our cameras. In such cases, I moved away. We tried to walk in groups, to join the Western journalists. These were the elementary precautions we took.

Now I am convinced that the threats were real, but I was unable to speak of it then, because it would look like the persecution complex.

After the so-called "referendum", my colleagues told me FSB officers met them and asked about me, about what I was doing. Whenever I was leaving the house, I felt people watching. I tried to meet my peers some-where in the park on the benches, somewhere in a public place.

However, after the "referendum", some changes occurred, the overt threats from the side of the pro-Russian activists ceased, and attacks on journalists became less frequent. In May, I took my family back to Simfe-ropol. I hoped that explicit mayhem would stop and we would be able to work.

Actually, then we started working as a full-fledged editor's office. We were ten. We launched a website. We leased a room in Oktiabrskyi office center. We kept our hardware there and videographers sometimes edited their materials there.

However, when the guys came to work in the morning, they noticed that some things were displaced. Someone was delving into our things.

We worked openly, we had a Radio Liberty logo on the microphone, we had the appropriate ID and introduced ourselves as Krym. Realii jour-nalists. Nevertheless, we weren't let in the parliament, the government, and other authorities any longer. At public events, the police started catch-ing our reporters. We were not talking about it publicly then.

The main editorial computer was in my home. I was sitting at my apartment in May, with my window open, watching the people travelling by. Then FSB scaled up its activities, searching some fellow journalists, so I, should anything happen, was ready to run into the next room with an open window facing the garden, and to throw the computer into the bushes of currants and raspberries growing under the window, should the FSB come."

The activities of Krym. Realii editor's office was covered by the Cri-mean media, which were closely controlled by the new Russian government.

On November 21, 2014, *Krymskie Izvestia* published an article[9] by Yuriy Portov *"There are lots of homo among us, but sapiens are miss-ing."* It reproduced the Russian propaganda theses: USA hates Rus-sia, Krym. Realii journalists sold out because they are paid by the US Congress, Crimea was outside its home country and now is

---

9   Y. Portov. There are lots of homo among us, but sapiens are missing / Krymskie Izvestia, 21.11.2014. URL: http://crimiz.ru/index.php/2011-03-13-12-08-25/16936-2014-11-21-06-49-43

back, the journalists' ideas are dictated by NATO, and the Kama Sutra is mentioned in jest.

Ru4ssian soldiers in Crimea. Photo by Stanislav Yurchenko (RFE/RL)

"Let's take, for example, the electronic media, says the article, Krym. Realii. *It's better, of course, not to take. But let's overcome the cleanliness and think philosophically. These Krym. Realii were born at the Radio Liberty. And the money to Radio Liberty is given by the Congress of the United States. And the authorities of the United States hate Russia. And Crimea returned to Russia, having belonged to Ukraine after 60 years as a present. So what realities, do you think, can be in Krym. Realii?*

For example, the ex-Minister of Resorts of Crimea "philosophizes" about the holiday season in Crimea. The idea is simple: it's bad for me without you, beloved Crimea, to fly with one wing. The philosophical question to the "secondhand-Minister", where would Crimea be, if it failed to reach its Mother Russia?

Or a former Ukrainian political reporter, who suddenly left Ukraine, shares his "philosophical" opinion. The idea is similar. I can see everything from above, you must know it. And continues thinking... But on top — in the bottom is from Kama Sutra, and these ideas are dictated by the guys from NATO."

On September 18, 2014, the same newspaper, Krymskie Izvestia, published an article[10] *"Write, Kolia, write,"* where the author exposes those Crimean journalists who did not trek to the office of the occupier. He writes overtly rude things. In particular, about those who cooperate with Krym. Realii:

"Here came the time, easy-going about conspiracy, to create an electronic media resource, a kind of "subsidiary" of Radio Liberty / Free Europe, to place it in Kyiv, not yet all in a muck, and smear, smear, smear shit on all what is happening in Crimea. And the role of "smearers" is quite familiar to our heroes.

And smelly liquid streams started flowing from Simferopol to Kyiv in email and SMS. However, it was too scary to subscribe their "famous" names, so few readers of the hastily fabricated website use simple and straightforward pseudonyms. I would like to reassure the "fighters invisible front" and tell them, "write, Kolia write. Your verbal liquid stool will serve as fertilizer in the new Russian Crimea for our future achievements. You just need to be careful about the way of getting the royalties. Russian laws are harsh and merciless to those who receive unearned income in foreign currency. Don't you agree that the things you are doing are anything but work"."

The critics of somebody else's aliases subscribed his own article using the alias Trofym Ohloblia. Sources say that this is a long-used alias of the chairman of the so-called "Public Chamber" of Crimea, Grygoriy Ioffe, who used to serve as the Deputy Speaker of the Crimean autonomous republic within Ukraine. And Ioffe alluded to the author of Krym. Realii, Mykola Semena, who was later arrested by the FSB.

Similar publications appeared in different media fairly regularly.[11]

---

10   Write, Kolia, write! / Krymskie Izvestia, 18.09.2014. URL: http://crimiz.ru/index.php/2011-03-13-11-38-40/16208-2014-09-18-06-06-34

11   See, e.g.: Yu port. Nightingales grunted / Krymskie Izvestia, 20.09.2014 URL: http: //crimiz.ru/index.php/2011-03-13-11-38-40/16262-2014-09-22-06-04-13; Y. Portov. Twerp Ivan Ampilogov Trying to Steal Dostoevsky' laurels / Krymskie Izvestia, 06.12.2014. URL: http://crimiz.ru/index.php/2011-03-13-11-38-40/17220-2014-12-11-12-04-28

"FSB officers invited to the trusting interview and just said that it was dangerous for you to work with Krym. Realii. That they were American spies."

"Such an environment was created, says Volodymyr Prytula, *that we had no other choice. We decided to move the editor's office outside of Crimea. Two editors left for Kyiv. I first went to Chaplynka, the closest town of Kherson region to Crimea.*

But this is a small town, the border with Crimea is not protected, anything could happen. So we decided to settle in Kherson. During the summer and autumn of 2014, I brought my family there. However, there was a threat of the Russian invasion in the south of Ukraine. So in the end, we decided that the editor's office should be located in Kyiv.

About a dozen journalists still work with us. However, they are subject to continuous pressure. For example, the so-called "preventive meetings" are held. FSB officers invite us to trusting interviews and just said that it was dangerous for you to work with Krym. Realii. That they were American spies. That Prytula is an American spy. He went away and left you to the wolves. You are the cannon fodder here. You will have problems if you work. If not you, then your relatives.

It was known than that some people in Crimea have gone missing. Therefore, FSB officers' advice was: „You'll come out of the house, and be gone? Family will cry and search for you. Think about whether you need it."

They called our colleague, whose husband was doing business. They say: "We know that your husband is in business." This was a clear hint. Then the family told her to cease cooperating with us. Now she left journalism and is engaged in the advertising business."

After the editor's office moved to Kyiv, the Russia-appointed government did not stop its persecution of Krym. Realii journalists. On April 20, 2016, the chairman of the so-called "Council of State" of Crimea, Volodymyr Konstantinov, called the journalists of Krym. Realii the enemies of the "Republic of Crimea". *"I know these people very well,* TASS news agency cited[12] him. *They are our enemies. They*

---

12   The speaker of the State Council of Crimea called the journalists of the Internet publication Krym. Realii the enemies of Russia / TASS, 20.04.2016. URL: http://tass.ru/politika/3222905

are the enemies of Russia, the enemies of Crimea. Whatever they wrote, they have only one purpose, to hurt us, to do us bad," said Konstantinov.

According to him, the materials published in such editions have nothing to do with journalism and freedom of speech. *"It has nothing to do with freedom of speech at all. There is no freedom there. There is only lies. It is paid for by Western intelligence agencies with one purpose, to harm Russia. Whatever we do, they will continue looking for something nasty. Please, do not confuse it with freedom of speech,"* added Konstantinov.

This is how he commented on accusations of the Crimean reporter of Krym. Realii, Mykola Semena, by the FSB in appeals to violate the territorial integrity of Russia. Within Semena's case, seven journalists who worked with Krym. Realii were searched. In the autumn of 2017, Semena was sentenced by the occupation court. Learn more about this case written in one of the following sections.

On April 20, 2016, Krymskaya Pravda published an article[13] by Nadiya Valuyeva entitled "Focus on Magadan." The title contained a hint that the accused reporter of Krym. Realii Mykola Semena will go to Magadan, where Stalin's Gulag camps were located. The author, referring to the Russian NTV reporter Oleg Kriuchkov, accused Volodymyr Prytula of spying in favor of US and Ukrainian special services. Besides, the author said that Russia intends to block Krym. Realii completely.

"However, as we were reported by the prosecutor's office of the republic, wrote Valuyeva, *they "collect the materials for the Prosecutor General's Office of RF and further to Roskomnadzor to close Krym. Realii information service. This is a malicious service, their publications contain the justification of sabotage, extremism and infinite discrediting of the authorities in Crimea, inciting ethnic hatred.*

Earlier, the prosecutor's office of the Republic of Crimea initiated the issue of blocking certain publications of Krym. Realii aimed at discrediting Russia's activities in the Republic of Crimea, inciting international and

---

13   N.Valuyeva. Focus on Magadan / Krymskaya Pravda, 20.04.2016. URL: http://c-pravda.ru/newspapers/2016/04/20/kurs-na-magadan

ethnic hatred and calling for extremist activity." The author's stylistics is preserved.

At the extended board of the so-called "prosecutor's office" of Crimea "prosecutor" Natalia Poklonska told about blocking, but not only with respect to Krym. Realii. She said that during 2015, her Office found extremist materials on 54 websites.

On February 13, 2016, the editor's office of a popular Ukrainian website Ukrainska Pravda received a notice from the Russian regulator Roskomnadzor on restriction of access to the resource *"in the information and telecommunications networks, including on the Internet, based on the requirements of the Prosecutor General's Office of RF dated September 30, 2015"* because of the notice, which *"contains calls to riots, extremist activity, participation in mass (public) events held in violation of the established order."* This happened after the editor's office, at the request of the same Roskomnadzor, did not remove news in which the MP of Ukraine Refat Chubarov allegedly urged Ukraine to open war against Russia.

The same month, the Ukrainian websites Censor.net and Apostrophe were blocked. Later the practice of blocking the websites expanded. They blocked the websites of Krym. Realii, 15 minut, Sobytiya Kryma, Meridian Sevastopol, Chornomorka TV channel, Obozrevatel, ATR TV channel, Krym SOS NGO, UAinfo, STB, Hromadske Radio and others.

On July 29, 2016, the "prosecutor's office" of Crimea announced that it intends to restrict access to 60 Internet resources. To this end, it prepared and sent to the Prosecutor General's Office an opinion that 60 Internet resources contain urges to extremist and other illegal activities. It was also reported that at the request of the "prosecutor's office" of Crimea, four books were included in the federal list of extremist materials.

> "Russia's practice is very similar to fighting of the communist Soviet Union with Radio Liberty or Voice of America. However, it is adjusted for time."

One of the reasons for restricting access to websites, according to the so-called „prosecutor's office" of Crimea, is the decree of the „prime minister" of Crimea Serhiy Aksionov 30 January 2015 „On approval of the Comprehensive Plan to counter terrorist ideology in the Republic of Crimea for 2015-2018." According to this document, „the ideology of terrorism shall mean a series of ideas, concepts, beliefs, dogmas, targets, slogans, justifying the need for terrorism and other destructive ideas, that have led to or may lead to such an ideology."

Thus, not only acts, but also thoughts and ideas are persecuted and restricted. This definition is vague, has no clear legal framework; this leads to the fact that the FSB or the "prosecutor's office" subjectively determine whether the idea is destructive or not.

"Russia's practice, says Volodymyr Prytula, *is very similar to fighting of the communist Soviet Union with Radio Liberty or Voice of America. However, it is adjusted for time. Given the new realities, they use the old methods next to the new ones. But you must remember what came out of the Soviet Union destroying freedom of speech. An ultimate defeat."*

Reporter-"Extremist" Mykola Semena

On April 19, 2016, disturbing news spread around Ukrainian media: seven Crimean journalists in different parts of the peninsula were searched.

The veteran of Crimean journalism Mykola Semena had been charged by the occupation authorities, which punish with up to five years in prison. A year and five months later, on September 22, 2017, the journalist was sentenced to two years in prison and three years of ban to engage in professional activities. Later on, the supreme court reduced the ban to engage in professional activities by one year, from three to two years.

He was charged with calling to violate the territorial integrity of Russia using the media. He allegedly has made such a call in an article on the website of Radio Liberty project, Krym. Realii.

Mykola Semena, a man of retirement age, has worked as a reporter of Den Ukrainian newspaper in Crimea for nearly twenty years and cooperated with Radio Liberty. Radio Liberty project, Krym. Realii, was established after Russia illegally annexed Crimea. In addition to the staff, it had a chain of freelancers.

Mykola Semena was sentenced to two and a half years of probation. After completing his sentence, he moved to Kyiv. Photo by Alina Smutko (RFE/RL)

"I realize how much energy, effort, and money from the state budget they have spent for my humble person, and I feel terribly, says Mykola Semena. *They used electronic surveillance, intercepted my phone, sent tails after me, took pictures of me, intentionally sent people to install a spy app on my computer. This campaign involved several dozen people. And all this was not for the killers, saboteurs, terrorists. All this was for a single article or, to be more precise, for a couple of paragraphs from it.*

Does it make sense for the secret services to arrange the tracking of journalists, to intercept their mail and their phones and to waste huge sums of taxes when they can buy a newspaper at a kiosk for pennies or regularly read the news sites to keep track of who is writing about what?

If all these resources and actions were focused on good things, they could move mountains. But no! They are spent on the comprehensive surveillance of society, turning Russia, as I see it in annexed Crimea, into the police state."

> "This article is a ban to engage in professional activities, unseen in the democratic world."

In December 2013, the State Duma of Russia introduced a new article into the Criminal Code, Article 280.1. It provided for liability for public calls to violate the territorial integrity of Russia. It has entered into force on May 9, 2014. In just two and a half months, on July 21, 2014, the State Duma adopted amendments to the said article aggravating the liability for its violation.

After amendments, the incitement to violate the territorial integrity of Russia using the media provides for a punishment by *"compulsory labor for up to four hundred and eighty hours, subject to a disqualification to hold certain positions or to engage in certain activities for up to three years, or imprisonment for up to five years, subject to a disqualification to hold certain positions or to engage in certain activities for up to three years."*

Mykola Semena considers that the introduction of this article is an employment ban (berufsverbot):

"The lawyers call this article "Crimean."

Its implementation has shown that Russia has been preparing not only the foci of the "fifth column" in Crimea and its armed forces to capture the peninsula in advance, since 2013 or earlier, but also introduced targeted amendments to its legislation so that it could "lawfully" bring to justice those who would disagree with the Russian version of the annexation.

Part 2 of this article, which I was charged with, provides for imprisonment of up to 5 years and a required ban of public activities. The article is designed so that not only to punish the one who would not agree with the annexation by a rather long prison term, but also to forbid him to speak to the media and make him shut up, close his way to the publicity.

Thus, for the journalists, this article is berufsverbot, unseen in the democratic world."

Criminal cases on similar charges have been initiated previously against two other Crimean journalists, **Andriy Klymenko** and **Anna Andrievska**, but they were staying in Kyiv when these cases were initiated. And Mykola Semena remained in Simferopol, so he was within the reach of occupation authorities.

Radiosvoboda, org   *Kusto,*

Caricature from Radio Liberty. Picture of Mykola Semena with the slogans: "I have a right to express my opinion," and "Crimea is not a part of Russia under international treaties".

His case has become the ultimate expression of the occupiers' fight against freedom of speech in Crimea. Russia has been taking comprehensive steps to squeeze free journalism from the peninsula in order to prevent the leakage of the truth about what was happening in the occupied peninsula.

Soon after the search, Mykola Semena said that the FSB was searching for a single article published on the website of Krym. Realii.

"It happened before seven o'clock in the morning when my wife woke me up and said that they came for a search. I did not have time to get up and make my bed, when masked men and some civilians, one of whom introduced himself as an investigator, rushed into my office. The others were the witnesses, whom they brought with them, including an IT expert.

The investigator, who called himself Vyacheslav Pyzin, showed me the ruling on the search and offered me to give weapons, drugs, computers and magnetic media voluntarily. I said I had no weapons or drugs, and my computers were there, so they could examine them. A man in civilian clothes, indicated in the search record as "expert", started their analysis.

This "expert" looked into my spare computer which I left on the table, having replaced my basic one with it. I invented such a naive way to defend myself. He almost shouted, "That's a different computer!"

During the investigation, I realized that this "expert" has been following the work of my computer every day (!) for about a year and knew its contents. He exposed my trick easily by the order of the folders in Explorer. The quickly found my work computer in the office and he restored the pieces of my articles using a special app, though I deleted them beforehand. He was looking for a certain article, the one which became the ground for the criminal case. It was called „Blockade, the Required First Step Towards the Liberation of Crimea."

> "I hugged my wife, not knowing whether to say goodbye or not. Relatives put some money in my pocket, just in case, and we left."

The „expert" fumbled in my computer and said, „Now let's find the memory card of a certain brand and a certain number." Soon, from behind the books, they removed the memory card with my archive of articles, which were all written by me for Den and Krym. Realii for almost two years. Moreover, there were contracts, monthly reports, official and private letters, memos to the editor's office and so on. Having found all this, the "expert" said, "I finished my job!" Also, he checked my phones and the investigator began to make the search record.

After that, I was allowed to wash and shave myself. Then they took me to the FSB office at Ivan Franko Boulevard, which housed the SBU until recently.

I managed to call my peer, Lilia Budzhurova, and asked to talk to some counsel and ask him to come to the office and give me a piece of advice. She said that counsel Emil Kurbedinov was waiting for me there already, and I thanked her for her help. Leaving the room, I hugged my wife, not knowing whether to say goodbye or not. Relatives put some money in my pocket, just in case, and we left.

> "It became clear that the security officers tried to cover the entire network of journalists preparing materials for the website of Krym. Realii."

This trip was quite alarming. I never traveled like this. People in masks and camouflage with guns were sitting in the van next to me sat, presuming no joke or liberties. We arrived at the office through the back entrance, and entered in not from the street, but from the yard. They did not seize my phones and documents. I was able to call my counsel, he obtained a permit, and soon I met Emil Kurbedinov in the corridors of the FSB.

That day, I was not the only victim of searches and detention. When I managed to call Budzhurova, I asked if someone else was searched. She said that besides me, a total of seven of our fellow journalists were being searched not only in Simferopol, but also in other cities. She named names.

These were people who had to do with Krym. Realii. Therefore, it became clear that the security officers tried to cover the entire network of journalists preparing materials for the website.

There were the camera reporter, photo editor, Internet content manager, report authors, reporters, and even the office manager since the days when we still had an office. I have seen some of them here through the open doors in other rooms, where they were interrogated by the other investigators, or accidentally met them in the corridor, though our convoys tried to prevent such meetings and did not allow us to communicate with each other. I realized that all of those who were searches were here already, and all of them were questioned.

> "It was intimidation of Crimean journalists in an attempt to separate them from cooperation with Kyiv publications. Consequently, most of those who cooperated with Radio Liberty in terms of freelance were immediately dismissed from their principal employment places in Crimea. Their management was just scared."

I recalled that during the search, the phone of the investigator Vyacheslav Pyzin was ringing frequently. From his words during a telephone conversation, I realized that some people told him how the searches with other journalists were passing, what they managed to find, and inquired of him what to do next.

Unit of the so-called "self-defense of Crimea" in Simferopol.
Photo by Stanislav Yurchenko (RFE/RL)

Clearly, they were investigators who conducted parallel searches of my colleagues. They called him, and he coordinated their work. Pyzin was my investigator, and a criminal case was instituted against me only, while my colleagues were the witnesses.

Later I read the authorization to search my colleagues. It noted that the evidence of my journalistic work and my collaboration with Krym. Realii should be sought. Therefore, they seized the computers and other materials of my colleagues related to Krym. Realii.

I am sure it was intimidation of Crimean journalists in an attempt to separate them from cooperation with Kyiv publications. Consequently, most of those who cooperated with Radio Liberty in terms of freelance were immediately dismissed from their principal employment places in Crimea. Their management was just scared. Because of the seizure of their office equipment, they were forced to suspend their journalistic activity.

Nothing fancy was found at my peers, and they didn't say anything important to the investigators during interrogations. Most of them resorted to the article of the Constitution of Russia on the right not to incriminate oneself, and the investigation or prosecution didn't even enter any of them in the list of witnesses to be interrogated in court. Some of them came to the court only to sympathize with me, for which I am eternally grateful to them.

The "KGB" paralyzed the network of Crimean reporters for some time. However, it was restored fairly quickly, and the website began to publish relevant and accurate information about Crimea again, including information received on site. Journalism was not scared of the intelligence service."

The "prosecutor" of Crimea, Natalia Poklonska, appointed by the Russian authorities, said that the journalists justify extremists and terrorists. *"The journalist is prosecuted on the grounds of paragraph 2 of Article 280.1 of the Criminal Code of the Russian Federation. This journalist has prepared and published an article containing statements intended to violate the territorial integrity of Russia, which is not allowed neither to reporters nor to anyone else,"* she said on the day of searches.

She didn't call the name of Mykola Semena, but all those concerned were aware of whom she meant. Poklonska said that the publication was devoted to the blockade of Crimea by Ukrainian activists.

"They actually justify the actions of extremists and terrorists. We would not allow crimes against Russian citizens and Russia as a whole. The status of the journalist obliges us to adhere to the legal requirements," added the "prosecutor" of occupied Crimea.

Recalling the interrogation, Mykola Semena says that he was not going to give up the authorship of the article on the Crimea blockade. He believes that their confidential conversation with the counsel was overheard:

"My counsel Emil Kurbedinov and I asked the investigator to provide us with a confidential environment for the conversation, as stipulated by law. He took us into some ill-equipped room with holes in the walls, with

partitions, with a table and only one chair, as well as an auxiliary table with an electric kettle thereon.

We realized that we were still overheard or recorded or even shot. However, we needed to produce some strategy for the first interrogation and our relationship, so we continued to talk in a whisper. Soon after us, a tall burly man abruptly entered the room, and sharply turned on the kettle. Then he left in silence.

We can only guess what else what else was turned on in this room simultaneously with the kettle, since why else would an employee break into a room for confidential conversations between counsels and detainees and turn on the kettle during their talk?

It made no sense to give up the authorship of the article on Krym. Realii, and I didn't want to do it. I knew I had not committed any crime. Therefore, I agreed with Kurbedinov that I would admit the authorship of this text during the first interrogation. However, I would declare that it complies with international law. I will stress that I, while taking part in international discussion, have exercised the right to freedom of expression, information and freedom of opinion. Moreover, the text was published in the column for private thoughts. This is what I said during the interrogation.

The investigator chose the travel restriction as a precaution measure. Fortunately, I was not arrested. Somewhere at three or four o'clock, we left the office of the security service.

After the first interrogation, we decided that we should let the investigators demonstrate their skills. Not to help them, I will resort to the provisions of Article 51 of the Russian Constitution giving the right not to incriminate oneself.

Not to mention, the part of neighbors who sympathized with me was startled. After I returned, they all came to me and questioned me how and what. They mentioned that just on the eve of the search, they noticed suspicious persons at our street. They left their car away around the corner and walked down the street, looking around and studying the situation, room peculiarities, location of buildings and other passages. Clearly, this was intelligence collected by the security forces, who studied the location of the proposed campaign.

Later, the neighbors pointed out to me that a few days after the search; an unknown car was parked at our street day and night, with a

DVR directed toward our house. This car has been standing there for a week or more.

From time to time, a man came to it. He left somewhere for a short time, perhaps, changed the memory cards or batteries in the DVR, then returned and left the car at the same place.

Later, the Crimean Tatar Avdet newspaper published the observations of the residents of other places where the searches and arrests were held. They said that on the eve of searches, the territory was surveyed, and after searches, the cars with continuously working DVRs were left there.

This was the usual practice of the security services at the residence of the repressed people. Based on these signs, the Crimeans have learned to identify the places of the possible next-day searches, and knew that thereafter they should not show high activity near the houses of the searched people, or demonstrate ties with those who fell under suspicion to their camcorder."

> "Earlier, the repressive actions in Crimea were directed against one or two journalists, said the statement, and now the Russian authorities searched seven representatives of the journalistic profession."

The story of Mykola Semena has not gone unnoticed in the world. The Congress of the European Federation of Journalists, held in Sarajevo on April 25-26, adopted a statement[14] under the eloquent title *"Repression against Journalists in Crimea Reaching a New Level."*

"The Russian authorities searched seven representatives of the journalistic profession. One of them, an ex-reporter of the Ukrainian newspaper Den, a retiree Mykola Semena, was charged with calling for the violation of the territorial integrity of the Russian Federation. He faces five years in prison", read the statement.

The Council of Europe Committee to Protect Journalists also assessed the developments in Crimea as extremely dangerous for journalists. It published a new, top-level warning, about the danger for journalists in the Russia-occupied Crimea.

---

14   European Federation of Journalists declared that repression of journalists in the Crimea reached a new level / Telekrytyka, 27.04.2016. URL: http://detector.me dia/community/article/114694/2016-04-27-evropeiska-federatsiya-zhurnalistiv -zayavila-shcho-represii-proti-zhurnalistiv-u-krimu-viishli-na-novii-riven/

"Leaving Crimea or stopping to work would mean surrendering in terms of actual war."

Mykola Semena says that he was sure that they would come for him. Still, he consciously continued to work for Ukrainian publications:

"When sometime in late 2014 or early 2015 in Crimea it was announced that the Russian cyber troop battalion was stationed in the peninsula, and its job was later praised by the Defense Minister Sergei Shoigu, I realized that sooner or later they would come for me.

However, leaving Crimea or stopping to work would mean surrendering in terms of actual war. Besides, I realized that the editor's offices of Den and Krym. Realii rely on me as a source of local information and by value as a journalist is that I can watch all the events, their development and consequences here, on the site, and can assess everything from the point of view of the Crimean people. This is why all editor's offices of the world have their own reporters in the regions.

It was all the more important to continue to work in the situation where the Russian authorities took all means to distribute the information about the situation in Crimea, sugar-coated and advantageous to them, worldwide. The liar channels were created and brought even to the satellite, involving the radio and propaganda websites, and a lot of Russian propagandist reporters were sent to the peninsula.

On the other hand, to prevent the leakage of information unwanted for them, collaborators displaced all independent media from Crimea, and banned the delivery of Ukrainian newspapers and magazines to Crimea. Instead, they filled the kiosks with Russian printed products.

Besides, they distributed among business leaders and organizations the official secret lists of journalists and the media, to which it was strictly forbidden to provide any information and to invite them to any event. Dozens of our peers from this list were not allowed at the press conferences, were not give an opportunity to ask questions to officials, were not provided press releases and other information, and were not responded to requests for information.

"In such circumstances, stopping work would mean to show cowardice... I certainly understood the risk to which I exposed myself, but the journalistic professional duty outweighed the personal safety considerations."

In March and April, several foreign journalists' groups were robbed and beaten. Journalists were detained, searched, and beaten quite often. In other words, the Russians have taken steps to cut off the world from the true, independent information from Crimea completely.

Therefore, in such circumstances, stopping work would mean to show cowardice and to desert the colors of work, which is desperately needed by the editor's office. I certainly understood the risk to which I exposed myself, but the journalistic professional duty outweighed the personal safety considerations.

Mykola Semena at work. Photo by krymr.org (RFE/RL)

I should say that in February-March-April 2014, we had absolutely different conditions and ideas of the journalists' work. While in Ukraine, we got accustomed to freedom of speech, to the fact that the journalists were provided any information, that journalists were pursued sometimes, but it was not a government policy and a systemic phenomenon. We could make a dust and force the pursuers to give up. No one hid nor shied away from us.

We had the illusion that at least some freedom of speech would remain after the annexation. Therefore, the office of the Radio Liberty project Krym. Realii was created in Simferopol in these months. Radio Liberty has entered into a formal lease, all project journalists were accredited, and used the communications.

However, we soon noticed that a camcorder was installed right above the office door, recording who and when comes there, and that our phones started "failing" suspiciously and quite often. Therefore, the office was moved to another location soon, and ultimately closed to guarantee the safety of journalists.

In fact, regular journalism in Crimea was disrupted by the new government during the first months of the occupation, and was replaced by a system of purposeful misinformation and propaganda about the state of affairs in Crimea.

Incidentally, one of the collaborators, the so-called "Chairman of the Public Chamber" of Crimea Grygoriy Ioffe said that Krym. Realii is cut off from the information provided by Crimea. The matter is only that, he said, there are still a few journalists on the peninsula, whose strength is that they are all on site, see and dare to write everything as it is. However, he said, "we know their "handwriting" and can quickly determine who wrote it."

From these words, it was obvious that they did not care whether what was written was true or not, but rather who dared to write it. The main objective of the collaborators was to identify the true authors of publications, which they considered dangerous for their authorities. Therefore, in fact, the searches on April 19, 2016, and this criminal case meant for them a completion of a special operation to neutralize the chain of independent journalists.

What could we oppose to this? Actually, nothing. We, the journalists, were not taught the rules of secrecy, we did not have the means of protecting our computer or phone information channels. Our weakness, and still our advantage was that we were not spies but journalists, doing our journalism, not spy work. But we were not even allowed to do that.

Meanwhile, guided by common sense, my peers and I still took some measures. I, for example, made a backup archive of my materials on a separate memory card, which I was hiding behind the books on the shelf, and began to remove my work computer from the table at night, leaving a spare one, just in case of a sudden search. However, subsequent events have shown that under total surveillance, these measures are not effective.

We started subscribing our materials with aliases, though during the first few months in Den I was using my own name. This did not help, however. By the style of writing the materials, which was too hard to change, the "observers" from the Crimean authorities quickly unscrambled aliases and revealed the true authors.

On this basis, the local press opened a real smear campaign against us, independent journalists and outrageous persecution by those "peers" who have worked with us throughout the entire Ukrainian period, but now have become collaborators and went to serve the enemy.

It is a professional crime, because they are not only traitors to the interests of the Crimean people; they became the creators of the information myth on the "happiness" of Crimea as a result of the annexation. In each program and on each page they were deceiving their friends, fellow villagers, compatriots, assuring them of the benefits of life under the power of the aggressor country. These are the people who will never return to real journalism, since the lie they skillfully mastered is a different profession.

> "When the Crimean "secret police" chased journalists and fake terrorists, the real terrorists detonated their bomb in the underground in St. Petersburg, and the secret police were powerless to prevent it."

Shortly before the search, I wrote and published an article in Krym. Realii about the fact that the intelligence work of the Russian secret services against journalists is actually a manifestation of the KGB's incompetence, since they choose an easy way. Instead of catching real spies, terrorists and separatists, they chased journalists, who cannot and should not hide or keep up. It is not a part of their duties, and does not meet their legal status.

Instead, they always become easy prey for secret services, especially in totalitarian states — read newspapers, the internet and "trump up" to them anything, extremism, terrorism or incitement to overthrow the government, if the article contains some criticism of the government entities. That's what they did.

Incidentally, at the time when the Crimean "secret police" chased journalists and fake terrorists, the real terrorists detonated their bomb in the underground in St. Petersburg, and the secret police were powerless to prevent it. And on November 1, 2017, the pipeline and power lines were blown up in the Yalta area, but the perpetrators have not been found yet. So whom should they chase, the journalists, the faithful Muslims, or the real terrorists?

So the work of the Russian security service in Crimea, in my opinion, was a real professional failure. For the whole period since February 2014 until now, they could only oppose themselves to the amateurs in the operational search business, and failed to disclose any real intelligence officer, no real secret subversive group. They were "catching" the journalists to whom they artificially "trumped up" extremism, or the phantom supporters of religious organizations, which not only committed no crime, but largely did not do anything in these imaginary groups.

For example, the Crimean organization Hizb ut-Tahrir did not exist even on paper, since there was no formal membership in it, but those who had the imprudence to assemble on a particular occasion someone at a party and to discuss a topic of religion, politics, or literature were enlisted to it. KGB officers installed "bugs" there in some unknown manner, and then accused them of extremism, although the accused did not do anything except hold philosophical conversations."

On May 3, 2016, the name of Mykola Semena was called at the World Press Freedom days in Helsinki. Speaking there, he was remembered, along with others, by the editor of the Krym. Realii project, Crimean journalist **Olena Yurchenko**. She spoke of him in the context of persecution of Crimean journalists, including shadowing them.

"The independent journalists in Crimea are shadowed. Russian security services physically block taking photos and shooting videos by independent journalists at public events. In Crimea, there is a common practice of denunciations of independent journalists, including by journalists of the pro-government media," said Olena Yurchenko.

Mykola Semena says that not only are journalists shadowed. In his view, the entire society came under total control.

He recalls the details of how he was shadowed:

"Once my colleagues from mainland Ukraine were going to come to Crimea. They wrote to me on Facebook asking to meet. I realized that when we meet, the security service would take them into focus and who knows whether they wouldn't be presented as the "Ukrainian saboteurs". In order not to expose them to great danger, I had to refuse, although it would be interesting for me to talk to them.

They did not understand me, and accused me of cowardice. After a visit to Crimea, they wrote an article saying that panic mastered Crimea.

Much of this was true, because this was the effect sought by the current Russian government. However, my peers did not understand the extent of this phenomenon. Probably, they did not realize that there was a real reason for fear.

Pro-Russian Cossacks' patrol in Simferopol Photo by Yuriy Lukanov.

Soon after their visit, the driver of the Zaporizhzhia nuclear power plan Yevhen Panov and other "saboteurs" of Ukraine were detained. They fell into this trap for little or no reason. The case was apparently spun out of thin air to accuse Ukraine of violating the Minsk agreements.

Later, our colleague, Ukrinform reporter Roman Sushchenko was arrested for "espionage" in Moscow. He worked in Paris, but according to the FSB, he was spying against Russia.

So, the Ukrainian colleagues could then be presented as much more "qualified" "saboteurs" than Panov and his fellow in this case. My colleagues had the chance to be the first on the list of "spies", had I met with them and unwittingly made them the object of surveillance. They could be qualified as "saboteurs" or "spies" at the discretion of the security service.

During the first months after the annexation, the Crimean people were trapped by a heavy press of total surveillance. It often had quite wild forms, especially when the mayhem was showed by the so-called "self-defense of Crimea".

It has become dangerous even to appear with a camera in the streets. Once I was crossing the square and made some general shots. Two "self-defense representatives" approached me right away, and requested me to produce my documents and the pictures I had taken. I said that taking pictures in open areas in the city could not be prohibited under Russian laws. They said that it was true in peacetime, and now, they said, it was war.

When I asked them to show their documents, one of them pulled out a sheet of plain paper reading that the representatives of the "self-defense" are permitted to carry out "examinations, searches, and apprehensions", signed by the "chairman of the Council of Ministers" of Crimea Aksionov. I explained that this officer had no power to authorize searches and detentions by structures not designed to do so, and this power was available only to law enforcement agencies. They again said that it was true for the peacetime only.

I pulled out my camera. One of them said, "You've got a good camera!" I saw a clear spark of interest in his eyes, and I realized that if they find something to nag at, they would confiscate it "on the altar of the revolution" with pleasure. They looked disappointed because the camera contained only a few shots of the square we were standing at, so they did not find anything secret or criminal there. They let me go.

I have seen the personal surveillance horror most clearly during the interrogation. The investigator told my counsel, "We were browsing the computer of this reporter remotely and found this article." He pointed to a stack of sheets of office paper about 40-50 centimeters high (no exaggeration!), from which the colored stickers protruded. These were the screenshots of my computer display. I realized that they had been watching me for many months.

> "The FSB had a remote display, parallel to mine. It switched on simultaneously with my computer, and a special person had been watching everything I did on it, making shots at the right time."

I recalled that once, about a year ago, my internet connection failed. I contacted my ISP. They insisted that I invited an expert to my home. I argued that the failure is not my side, rather somewhere on the line, but they would not even listen to me, saying that they would resume the connection only after I let the expert come.

I was actually forced to allow the expert in. The experts were two. One was just watching, while the other was digging in my computer. He looked into the folders, browsed my apps, and inserted a USB flash drive. He didn't even throw eye on the router and cables.

Probably, then he installed a spy app on my computer. Almost three of seven volumes of my case contained screenshots from my computer. When I was allowed to look them through, I realized that the FSB had a remote display, parallel to mine. It switched on simultaneously with my computer, and a special person had been watching everything I did on it, making shots at the right time.

I got the impression that the shots sometimes were made automatically. The criminal case contained as many as forty identical pictures of my open mailbox, and the picture contained the on-screen clock showing the time when the pictures were taken, and I saw that the picture photos were taken at a one minute interval. Forty times the same thing! Only a machine could do this. That's the height reached by the technical progress in the KGB!

Once their on-duty officer must have been a bit late, and when I turned off my computer, it suddenly broke, and the program showed me that the text on a remote display is not saved; save or disable the remote display. This is how I learned that my computer had a remote display. Certainly, I tried to disable it, but this option was not available in my machine, or someone had prudently disabled it. However, I did not realize what this meant for me. I got it only during the investigation.

After the deployment of the Russian cyber troops in Crimea, the secret service forced all ISPs of the peninsula to cooperate with them. Even the newspapers published articles saying that they forced all IT firms dealing with the Internet and other communication lines to buy and install special hardware to surveille the customers.

Since then, all Internet traffic in Crimea, as well as throughout Russia, had been recorded, filtered, analyzed for key words and other parameters, and this was done almost automatically. Later, in one of the volumes of my case, I saw the printouts from my ISP containing the entire chronology of my computer operation in the network for several months, and printouts of the telephone company with a list of my phone calls.

By the way, I'd like to add a funny little detail. The certificate said that I had unordinary phones, and read, "Mykola Semena uses portable

radio stations..." and their numbers and identification codes were indi-
cated.

I vividly imagined how in the investigators' fantasies I used these
"portable radio stations," going to the forest like 007 agent, throwing an
antenna onto the tree and shouted, "Go ahead."

> "Every time I went downtown I saw a "trail." If I entered a cafe and used its
> Wi-Fi to access the Internet, a "man in gray" always appeared at a nearby
> table."

Of course, all these details were included in the case only in order to pre-
sent the investigation as if I was not as ordinary journalist, but a spy who,
as their certificate read, "maintains illegal, sustainable contacts with sub-
versive elements abroad."

At trial, we had to refute the spy insanity of this outburst. We had
to prove that the reporter's contacts with his editor's office and his rela-
tionship with his university course mates, friends, family, and colleagues
are neither illegal nor subversive.

Every time I went downtown I saw a "trail." If I entered a cafe and
using its Wi-Fi to access the Internet, a "man in gray" always appeared
at a nearby table and, pretending indifference, took out a laptop and, prob-
ably, monitored all the traffic of this communication hub. So I could not
call or write anything that would not be intercepted by them.

The operative agents often documented my trips downtown. If I
agreed to meet with some of my friends, we certainly saw suspicious per-
sons nearby. They carefully pretended to be taking pictures of some places
where there was nothing interesting to shoot, but managed to focus the
camera and take pictures of us.

After these meetings, we often found our phones heavily discharged.
They say that today the operative agents have a technical capability to
switch on the microphone function on your or your interlocutor's phone.

Once I was on the brink of arrest. At one of the city streets, I acci-
dentally met one of my fellow photojournalists. We talked about various
things, including about the current place of employment. I uttered the
phrase "it is dangerous to write, I do not want to repeat Sentsov's fate." I
meant Oleg Sentsov, a Ukrainian documentary filmmaker, who was sen-
tenced to twenty years for alleged preparation of a terrorist attack.

Obviously, the whole interception system responded to Sentsov's name, a key word. When we parted, I noticed that I was photographed too often when walking.

A car stopped near me, a man jumped out, holding his telephone with its camera pointed at me. He asked me how to get to the railway station, though he was driving from the railway station side.

So-called "Self-defense of Crimea". Photo by Stanislav Yurchenko (RFE/RL)

Along the way, I went to a photo shop, and when I left, a young man rushed to me, holding a camera in some strange way, by a strap only. He asked me to take the picture of him against the background of the street.

I almost mechanically picked up his camera and then doubted whether I was doing right, but it was too late. My fingerprints were on the camera already. He began to pose, I lifted the camera to my eye and saw that it has an unusual viewfinder; everything was small and not like in a conventional camera. I pressed the button several times. When I returned the camera to him, he took it back without touching the body, for the strap.

Later I realized that in this way they captured by fingerprints and samples of biological material, because my sweat remained on the case. Also, they might have taken an identification picture of the iris pupil of my eye. It appears that such a technique of identifying people exists. A special camera could shoot not through the lens, but vice versa, to shoot the eye through the viewfinder. Who knows whether this is true, but the "photographer's" behavior was more than suspicious.

When I came to my bus stop, in a minute or two, a young man approached me somehow unusually, from behind, and asked me how to get to Semashko hospital. While I was explaining the way to him, he raised his hand in front of my face. I saw that he was holding a "key" of a rather unusual shape, with a camera or camcorder mounted thereon. I clearly saw the lens directed at me.

I looked around and saw that the same young people, who were at least eight, surrounded me. They were about the same height and dressed in about the same manner, so they were noticeable. I got prepared to being detained. However, this did not happen.

Perhaps the campaign coordinator, who received my picture from the "key", recognized me. Knowing that I had nothing to do with Sentsov, he realized that the investigators had mistaken me for somebody else and canceled the detention order.

I looked around once again and saw that all those who had surrounded me got scattered in different directions. The young man with a "key" quickly disappeared too, although not in the direction of Semashko hospital. Only later, when my inner tension loosened, I realized what could be the result of a simple mentioning of Sentsov name outdoors in terms of the comprehensive interception and surveillance.

After the opening of the criminal case and search until the trial commencement, I realized that at that point I had become a fairly well "documented and developed object" and, therefore, less interesting. I think that from then onwards the field surveillance of me was cancelled, but the telephone and Internet interception continued, and perhaps continues until today. During the trial, which lasted for almost 11 months, I have not felt such a consideration, although I saw the signs of computer and phone surveillance. However, it is true not only for me, but I think for all residents of Crimea, and everyone here will remain "on the hook" for a long time.

Moreover, I was given a lot more freedom than before. Many journalists came to the hearings, and my contacts with them were not only undesirable, but also needed for the special services. So they did not try to prevent them, and even promoted them. The fact is that during the trial, it is important for the authors of the criminal case to know the position of the defendant, its counsels, to understand their defense strategy and hear the possible evidence. How to do it? The preferred way is their interviews to journalists and talks to community activists.

Generally, a comprehensive recording and analysis of telephone traffic was introduced in Crimea. The curators from the security service were appointed to all editor's offices of the newspapers, television and radio, as well as internet sites, which have provided instructions and banned the use the terms such as "annexation", "occupation" and so on. They set detailed requirements for the subjects and direction of materials. In many editor's offices, the undercover agents were appointed. Subsequently, the entire staff was revised there. All media were re-registered under the Russian laws. In fact, censorship in various ways has returned to Crimea, which we have forgotten in Ukraine."

On July 12, 2016, OSCE representative on Freedom of the Media Dunja Mijatovic mentioned Mykola Semena in her statement. This was due to the publication of the "list of terrorists and extremists" from the Federal Service for Financial Monitoring of Russia in the Russian media.

Dunja Mijatovich. Picture from OSCE site. In 2014 OSCE Representative on Freedom of the Media (2010–2016).

"The list, which used to be confidential, reads the statement of Mijatovic, *includes the Crimean journalists, Mykola Semena from the online publication Krym. Realii and Anna Andrievska from the Center for Investigative Reporting."*

"The publication of this list may pose a threat to the journalists and threaten their security, says Dunja Mijatovic. Security of journalists is the responsibility of public authorities; they should not expose them to the risk of prosecution under suspicion within the law on combating extremism."

"I urge the relevant authorities to eliminate the list with journalists' names and to review their practice endangering those who exercise their right to freedom of expression, added Mijatovic. Labeling the journalist as a terrorist for his criticism and critical reports only cannot be justified."

That list also included the Crimean citizen **Andriy Klymenko,** editor in chief of the BlackSeaNews news agency. In general, it contained thousands of people, including the leaders of the Crimean Tatar people Ilmi Umerov, Refat Chubarov, Mustafa Dzhemilev and many others.

Mykola Semena recalls that listing all these people transferred them into the category of those who could not use any financial service in any financial institution or even mail.

"Soon after the start of the investigation, he says, I took my bank card and tried to withdraw money from an ATM. I was refused. The machine pointed to some error. I turned to the operations officer of the bank, and she told that I "match the list." She referred me to the bank central office for explanations.

They explained that according to the law on the prevention of terrorist financing, I was entered into the list of those who are prohibited to carry out any transaction in all financial institutions in Russia, other than social benefits, such as pensions. Everything else was prohibited. Of course, the bank could only give an explanation on the implementation of this resolution, but no one in the bank could explain who included me in that list and on what basis.

Later I learned that this resolution passed, and the list is prepared and updated by the organization called Rosfinadzor. However, I still do not know who and on what basis included me in that list. I was not given any response. This was not explained to Anna Andrievska or Andriy Klymenko, to Refat Chubarov, Akhtem Chyigoz or Ilmi Umerov, or thousands more people designated as terrorists. I was listed under number

4603, though now the number has changed, because the list is regularly replenished by new "terrorists."

I found "The list of terrorists and extremists (current)" on the Internet and saw that it included not only the defendants in all Crimean cases, but also a number of organizations, such as the Mejlis of the Crimean Tatar people, Bratstvo Ukrainian organization, Pravyi Sektor, Tryzub Imeni Stepana Bandery, Hizb ut-Tahrir, UNA-UNSO, the UPA and even Russkoye Natsionalnoye Edinstvo Riazan Municipal Public Patriotic Organization, Russkoye Natsionalnoye Edinstvo Omsk Organization of the Public Political Movement, Obshchina Korennogo Russkogo Naroda Schelkovskogo Raiona Moskovskoy Oblasti and thousands of others.

My counsel Aleksandr Popkov said that he and their civil rights advocacy group Agora in Russia were dealing with this list, but failed to do anything. It turns out that Russia simply took advantage of the International Convention on the prevention of terrorist financing. However, de facto, it defiled the same, since it includes people and organizations in the list not by court award, but arbitrarily for political motives, perhaps automatically after the institution of criminal proceedings, without waiting for their resolution and ultimate judgment."

Despite being under investigation, Mykola Semena did not confuse or became silent. He submitted a proposal to the international institutions to create a special international institution to protect civil liberties and human rights in Crimea. On September 22, 2016, Semena's address was read out in Warsaw at the OSCE annual conference on the human dimension in the West, at the Human Rights Information Center event, by his counsel Aleksandr Popkov, who worked with Emil Kurbedinov.

"The Crimean people shall be secured and guaranteed all civil liberties and human rights, read Semena's appeal. *However, this would not happen without the international legal monitoring of the progress of our cases and legal situation in Crimea.*

Ukraine's capabilities to protect its citizens in Crimea are limited by the Russian military presence and the refusal of defenders' access to the peninsula. Moreover, the scale of the Russian repression has reached such a level that it can be opposed by a wide international solidarity would bring of human rights defenders. It would be effective to creating an international legal framework to protect civil liberties and human rights in Crimea, which would take control of all politically motivated proceedings, would provide legal support to repressed activists, would take part in trials, and would publicize the information about all violations of human rights and civil liberties among the global community."

In the courtroom, Mykola Semena (in the center) with lawyers Aleksander Popkov (to the left) and Emil Kurbedinov (to the right). Photo by Anton Naumliuk (RFE/RL)

Mykola Semena believes that the whole trial with respect to his case was an eloquent illustration of the repression which Russia uses in Crimea in relation to those who disagree with the occupation.

"Russia's repression affected me personally, he said. However, unlike the cases of kidnapped and murdered activists, in my case, the occupation authorities sought to demonstrate the appearance of justice. The trial was organized with all relevant procedures. It was a trial in form. However, it was a political retaliation in fact. I did not admit my guilt and could never admit it."

The trial in the so-called "Zheleznodorozhnyi court of Simferopol" was built on the basis of three quotations from Mykola Semena's article, which he subscribed with his alias Valentyn Honchar. The article was devoted to the blockade of the peninsula, initiated by several members of the Ukrainian parliament and activists, which was intended to cease the supply of goods to Crimea from Ukraine and from Crimea to Ukraine. Strategically, the campaign initiators were aiming at de-occupation of the peninsula.

The court judgment contains three quotes from this article:

1. *"The blockade must be complete, comprehensive and designed to be immediately followed by the release. We block Crimea, and wait for its release. Before starting the blockade, care should be taken that the overwhelming majority of Crimean residents could hear the words of Kyiv. The president or the prime minister should address them, and explain the necessity of this step and its causes. The blockade should be the first step, a harbinger of release; it should be a clear military operation, and it must be accompanied by all required measures, including the operation to neutralize and disrupt the Russian ferry across the Kerch Strait, Russian communications, occupants' communication, and neutralization of the combat capability of their headquarters. The war must be conducted decisively, using military means. The blockade will be followed by the second phase, the complete liberation of Crimea."*

2. *"Therefore, Crimea has been under German occupation for 2.5 years only, and Kyiv should not allow Crimea to remain under the Russian occupation longer than under the German one. Less than a year is left! Otherwise, all shame!"*

3. *"Giving up Crimea does not mean giving up Ukraine, and it should return Crimea."*

The expert of the forensic department of the so-called "Russian FSB Office for the Republic of Crimea and Sevastopol City" Olga Ivanova concluded that the article contains the calls to violate the territorial integrity of Russia. Meanwhile, seventy-two (!) errors were found in the text of the linguistic examination opinion prepared by Ivanova. Later, another expert assessed her as a person who does not know the rules of the Russian language and suggested withdrawing her.

Mykola Semena's counsels requested to review the FSB opinion. The review was written by the PhD of Philology, graduate of Maksim Gorky Literature Institute Elena Novozhilova, who also has a lawyer's degree.

She noted: *"The expert has made a total of 72 errors in her language (on approximately ten pages), including 21 errors related to the higher philological education (university degree), 32 errors of the middle and high school level, and 15 errors of the elementary school level."*

Elena Novozhilova concluded: *"The expert who has prepared the opinion does not know the rules of the Russian language at the high school (expertise), or even at the secondary school level (general knowledge). Her written language is quite illiterate. Regardless of whether the expert has a higher philological education (the diploma details are not provided), she shows a lack of competence and shall be removed."*

Counsel Aleksandr Popkov asked an expert to provide the philological examination opinion on Mykola Semena's article. He formulated two questions:

"Does the international principle of territorial integrity apply to Crimea as a part of the Russian Federation in the current political environment?"
   "Can the statements in the text entitled "Blockade, the Required First Step towards the Liberation of Crimea" subscribed by "Valentyn Honchar, political analyst" contribute to a violation of the territorial integrity of the Russian Federation?"

The answers to these questions were provided by the Doctor of Political Science, Emeritus Professor of Kuban State University (Krasnodar, Russia) Mikhail Savva. He arrived at the following conclusion: *"The text comes from Crimea's belonging to Ukraine, and in this part, it is fully consistent with international law and contemporary international political practice. The above text cannot violate the territorial integrity of the Russian Federation, since Crimea is not a part of the RF. Therefore, public discussion about the belonging of any territory of the state is a manifestation of the right to expression and does not violate the territorial integrity, so the text entitled "Blockade, the Required First Step towards the Liberation of Crimea" subscribed by "Valentyn Honchar, political analyst" does not contribute to a violation of the territorial integrity of the Russian Federation."*
   Judge Natalia Shkolna ignored the defense and independent experts' arguments and found Mykola Semena guilty. She

sentenced him to two and a half year suspended sentence with a probation period of three years and a ban to engage in public activities.

Lawyer Emil Kurbedinov says that Mykola Semena was preparing for the worst before trial, „*Certainty, Mykola was worried and nervous. This is a normal reaction of a normal person. He is not a criminal, who used to play casemates and "cops".*

"We were hoping for some adequacy in this case. We hoped that he would not be imprisoned actually. During the trial in Crimea it happened that Server Karametov, an elderly man who went for a single picket, was put in prison for ten days. Mykola came up to me and said, "If they have put such an old and sick man in prison, they would certainly do it to me." And he began to ask what he should take with him, what spoons, underwear, asking how to behave in prison... After Karametov's conviction not only he, but many of us lost optimism, and Semena was mentally preparing for a term in prison.

Certainly, we are not satisfied with the ultimate judgment. And we do not want to get used to the fact that a conditional sentence was good news. However, thank God, they did not cross the line."

The OSCE Representative on Freedom of the Media Harlem Desir called the sentence to Mykola Semena a violation of freedom of expression and freedom of the media.

The EU Delegation to Ukraine also stressed that the European Union encourages removing all charges from Mykola Semena and immediately releasing all those detained in violation of international law.

The Ministry of Foreign Affairs of Ukraine protested against the judgment of the occupation court of Crimea.

Moreover, Mykola Semena himself is determined to bring his case to the European Court of Human Rights.

"I know that there is still a long way to go, says Semena. *But we're moving on, and we will win, since there is blunt force and absurd on their side, while there is truth and common sense on our side. The truth will ultimately prevail, sooner or later." Lawyer Alexander Popkov appealed to the*

European Court of Human Rights on March 27, 2018. The case had been registered under the number 15741\18.

"We asked about assigning priority to the case, since it was regarding the journalist, however we were refused, – Popkov said. – At this moment the case has not been communicated, i.e., it has not reached the stage when the court addresses questions to the state and the plaintiff."

Meanwhile on September 16, 2022, Russia officially ceased being a High Contracting Party to the Convention for the Protection of Human Rights and Fundamental Freedoms due to its expulsion from the Council of Europe. The European Court of Human Rights (ECHR) clarified that it is still competent to review the complaints directed against the Russian Federation related to its actions or inaction, provided that the contested events had occurred before September 16.

Popkov stated that during Mykola Semena's case Russia was still a member of the convention, which is why it was obliged to take responsibility for its actions. However, Russia will not contemplate paying compensation.

On January 14, 2020, a Russian occupation court granted Popkov's request regarding the early termination of the probation period and removal of Semena's criminal record. The journalist was finally able to leave for Ukraine's mainland.

"I was very nervous while approaching to the Chongar1 checkpoint", he remembers. "After the criminal case against me had been opened, I was included in the list of such entities as Russian Financial Monitoring. People, who end up in their list are usually the ones accused of terrorism, or the ones like me – of calls to violation of the Russian "territorial integrity".

Those who get pointed at by the prosecutor's office after the initiation of the criminal case, get in that list. And that means that they cannot use your bank account. They are not allowed to cross the border either.

My lawyer Alexander Popkov was discussing that with the prosecutor's office, since the initiation of the criminal case does not mean that the person is found guilty. It can happen only after the official court decision. However, in Russia they do not pay attention to that."

When the court decided to fulfil my request about the parole, I still acted as if I remained in that blacklist. Because there were zero guarantees that I had been excluded from it. In that case a purchase of bus tickets would mean that the selling company would have to immediately report about that to the FSB RF (The Federal Security Service of the Russian Federation). Therefore, they would be tracking my movement. And who knows which instructions they could have given, for example, to border officers.

That is why I made an agreement with one of my acquaintances and they gave me a ride to the checkpoint in their car. In my luggage I had two computers and three photo cameras, because I was about to leave for good and they could have questions to me. And I wasn't going to come back while Crimea is still under the occupation. I believed that it wasn't going to last forever, and a lot of Crimeans, including me, will have an opportunity to go back home.

But there were two girls sitting at the checkpoint. I put my cameras and phones into different suitcases. They scanned them with special equipment. And no questions arose.

You cannot imagine my feelings when I crossed to our side, where the Ukrainian flag was flying. Our people got intel about my crossing the border. I was met by SBU (Security Service of Ukraine) employees.

At the railway station in Kyiv friends and colleagues met Semena. He said that he could finally inhale the air of freedom again. He was walking the city without being afraid of being watched. According to his words, when there is freedom, people do not notice it. Freedom becomes noticeable when freedom is taken away.

Semena said that after the verdict, although he wasn't formally in prison, it was hard to say that he was free, too, for he was prohibited from any public activity.

"And this formulation is very vague: they could put any meaning into it if they wished" – he stated. – "For example, a speech in the library during the discussion of some book – can that be considered as a public activity or not? Or posting to Facebook, even not on political, but some neutral topic – would that be a public activity or not? Or can you take photos, for example of a wedding and then post these photos?"

The lawyer appealed to the judge, who put Semena on probation with a request to clarify the exact meaning of "public activity". She responded that everything is clear from the verdict. However, Semena believes that in fact it is not.

"After all, two and a half years of probation which I got as sentence would mean that if I broke the law, I would be locked up for those two and a half years of an actual term, plus additional punishment for a new violation" – he shares. *"That is why I had to be extra careful, so they would not set up against me and not send me to prison. I wrote a farewell post on Facebook, informing that there will be no further posts and explained the reasons".*

Psychologically you can imagine what it is like. It is like you are free but should limit yourself all the time. And for the journalist, who is a public person by profession and nature it is particularly difficult.

Semena recalled that after the search of his home on April 19, 2016, his friends suggested fleeing. Some people did so. For example, they went to Russia, then to Belarus and from there moved to Ukraine. Or to the Russian exclave of Kaliningrad, where you could get on a train that was heading through Lithuania, get off the train in Vilnius and seek asylum. However, Russians quickly forced Belarus, which remains friendly to them, to use the FSB "criminals" database. There were other ways of escape, but Russia blocked them too.

"You could also cross the border in a truck, hiding in boxes with potatoes" – he says – "But at that moment the way to Crimea for the trucks had already been blocked. Which meant that I was doomed to stay in Crimea.

After the trial, the surveillance was allegedly cancelled, however I was still noticing it. A friend from Kyiv was visiting me. We were sitting in a café, and he said that someone was watching us behind me. I turned around and saw that some man was taking pictures of us.

My phone and computer kept being monitored by FSB. On the Internet I found codes which allowed me to detect whether calls from my phones had been duplicated to another number. I entered those codes, and it turned out that yes – my calls had been redirected to a certain phone number. And that number was not Crimean, but some other, a Russian one.

There were also codes which supposedly allowed me to avoid phone calls being redirected. I tried to use them, but it didn't help. Which meant that FSB anticipated such attempts and could block them."

Twice a month Semena was obliged to visit the Federal Penitentiary Service, (the Russian abbreviation is FSIN). Being on probation, he needed to testify in person that he did not escape.

Every time he had to fill out a questionnaire about relationships with his family and neighbors, sources of livelihood, attitude to alcohol and drugs and so on. Besides that, so-called "educational conversations" were held with him, three times, about the harm of alcoholism.

"As they were about to do it for the fourth time" – Semena recalls – *"I could not take it anymore, so I said:*

'You are looking at my case. I had my gallbladder removed. The doctors categorically forbade me to drink alcohol. Which is why your lectures now are out the window.'

They replied that they had to re-educate me. However, you see, they weren't re-educating me, holding conversations about the Constitution and the right to freedom of expression. They walked all over it. Just as a pure formality, they kept speaking about things which had nothing to do with me.

Closer to the end of the term I requested to see my cases. I discovered that the probationers were supposed to be watched by the precinct inspector. Once in a quarter he had to visit the probationers, have conversations at their homes – with family, with neighbors. So, each time they wrote that the inspector was coming, but nobody was answering the door.

When right before the trial, where my appeal should have been considered, I paid a visit to the precinct inspector to get my testimonial, I told them my address. And he asked:"

'Do we even have such a street?'

Therefore, this declared nearly round-the-clock control on the FSB end is combined with purely formal fulfillment of duties on the end of the penitentiary service or even a complete ignoring of them. Perhaps it is related to the fact that the executives see the person – not a drunk, not a drug

addict, so why find fault with them? As for all those political aspects –
they are indifferent to them.

In the end Federal Penitentiary Service and precinct inspectors gave
me positive testimonials for the court. And I left there as soon as possible".

They Will Stay in Prison for Five Years

Retribution for "Krym" battalion

After the Crimea occupation, the journalist of the Center for Investigative Reporting **Natalia Kokorina** not only remained in Crimea, but also continued sending material from there. At the same time, she understood that they would come for her. However, the FSB visited her in the case of another colleague.

"For several months in a row I have been waking up at six in the morning, says Natalia. I got up from the bed and waited. If no one appeared until seven o'clock, I slept for another hour and finally woke up.

On March 13, 2015, I woke up at about eight; I was awakened by a call from an unknown number. I picked up the phone. The male voice introduced himself as the district police officer. He said that my parents' apartment door was broken. I had to arrive, because they had to leave the apartment. They could not leave until I arrive, because the door was open.

At first I was scared, since kidnapping cases had occurred already. People disappeared and did not return. Then, a few seconds later, I turned on the logic. I asked "Why did you go there?" – "We were called by the neighbors." – "And how did you get my phone number?" – "The neighbors gave it."

I know that none of the neighbors has my phone number. I realized that this is a search. I say, "Ok. I'm coming." I went there. On the way, I called my counterpart Serhiy Mokrushyn and described the situation. At the entrance, I was met by the FSB officer. He showed his identification and accompanied me to the apartment. He asked me to turn off my phone, took it away from me and put it on the shelf.

I was showed the ruling, according to which the search was conducted. It said that the search is a part of the criminal case opened after Anna Andrievska's article, which allegedly contained calls to violate the territorial integrity of the Russian Federation."

Early in the morning of March 13, 2015 in Kyiv, journalist **Anna Andrievska** received a call from her father residing in Crimea. Andrievska, who used to work in Argumenty Nedeli. Krym [ENG: Arguments of the Week. Crimea—ed.] newspaper moved to

Kyiv shortly after the so-called "referendum" on the status of the peninsula.

The phone call alerted Anna, because she usually communicates with her father via Skype. It appeared that he could not communicate with his daughter as usual, since the FSB representatives raided the house where Andrievska used to live with her parents and seized the PC. It was her father's PC.

FSB representatives presented the ruling of the court appointed by the occupiers saying that the journalist is charged in a criminal case under article 280.1 of the Criminal Code "Charges of public calls for the implementation of actions aimed at violating the territorial integrity of the Russian Federation using the media."

Such calls allegedly were contained in Andrievska's article "Krym Battalion Volunteers," published on[15] December 11, 2014 at the Center for Investigative Reporting. Thereafter, the special state institution Roskomnadzor blocked the website of the Center for Investigative Reporting.

"Early in the morning, when everyone was asleep, seven armed men in FSB uniform, some wearing ski helmets, broke into my parents' apartment, recalls Anna Andrievska. They asked whether weapons or drugs were at home. Of course, we have never had anything like that.

Then one of the security officials showed the ruling of the Simferopol court authorizing the search. That "document" stated that the search should be conducted in a criminal case instituted by the FSB under Article 280.1 of the Criminal Code due to the publication of "Krym Battalion Volunteers" at the Center for Investigative Reporting website. They took away this ruling, and did not leave a copy.

During the search, the security forces requested to give them all my personal belongings, including the family photos, which they also wanted to seize, but my parents prevented them. Since I have left this apartment about ten years ago, the FSB representatives had nothing special to seize. So, they took my old work notebooks from the pre-war period. They also removed all the equipment, although I have nothing to do with it; all these items belong to my parents."

---

15   A. Andrievskaya Krym Battalion Volunteers / Center for Investigative Reporting, 11.12.2014.URL: https://investigator.org.ua/articles/144257/

Andrievska tells that the security officers behaved insolently, „*They interrogated my parents, who had no counsel. The reproached my mother because she speaks Ukrainian, and requested that she speak to them in Russian only, asked why my parents brought up their daughter so badly, scared my grandmother and warned that they should sit quietly and not „scream blue murder.*“

A few months later, the father of Anna Andrievska was „invited“ to the FSB to take the seized equipment, and when he came, he was interrogated again for about six hours. He was shown a record of his telephone conversation with his daughter, and required to certify that he communicated with her. Also, the investigator tried to find out the details of Anna's professional career, place of residence and employment in Kyiv, as well as other details.

„*This interrogation was also conducted without a lawyer, and was accompanied by psychological pressure methods. The FSB investigator Maryna Savchuk reproached my father and said, „Your daughter is a Crimea traitor!“ It is very interesting to hear that from the person who betrayed the oath herself, having moved from SBU to FSB in 2014,*“ says Andrievska.

The editor in chief of the Center for Investigative Reporting Valentyna Samar believes that the institution of this criminal case had several reasons.

"*Firstly, she says, the rage of invaders was caused by the fact of publishing the material on three divisions of Crimean volunteers who are fighting in the ATO area, which breaks the myth that everyone in Crimea stands for Russia. After all, the article contains no phrase that could be classified as a "call to violate the territorial integrity of the Russian Federation."*

It's comical, but Roskomnadzor, justifying the decision to block the website of the Center for Investigative Reporting, which was started simultaneously with the criminal case of Anna Andrievska, wrote us that it treats the interrogative sentence at the end of material extremist! "Isn't it time to return it?" asks the journalist in the last sentence, referring to Crimea.

Moreover, this is material about the volunteers who helped the volunteer military units. They were three, and they were all called "Krym." This is the text version of the story broadcasted live in my "National

Security Issues" program at "Chornomorka" TV and Radio Company. The program was visited by Krym battalion commander Isa Akayev. He said in plain text that he will return Crimea and "will reach every" enemy and traitor.

So why was the criminal case opened based on the text version of the story? For me, the FSB rehearsed the practical application of Article 280.1 of the Criminal Code, which came into effect immediately after the annexation of the peninsula, and which provides for imprisonment, including for publications on the Internet, as was formulated there.

And, of course, it cannot be treated as a coincidence that the FSB investigator in this case was the former SBU investigator Maryna Savchuk, who changed colors. We knew her, because in 2012 she led the case of DDoS-attacks to the website of the Center for Investigative Reporting, opened by the SBU based on our statement during the parliamentary elections in Ukraine. The case for Andrievska's publication was a kind of a pilot case for the FSB in Crimea, followed by the other ones."

Valentyna Samar adds that it is a clandestine case, the hearings are held in camera, so none of the journalists knows his or her status and the current stage of investigation into the case.

Anna Andrievska says that the criminal case instituted against her affected several persons from her entourage, who also visited the hours of interrogation, although they know nothing about her professional activities. *"I was not called to the FSB for interrogation in person. No summons was served at the place of my registration in Crimea, and any attempt to learn more about the criminal case were unsuccessful,"* she said.

Subsequently, Andrievska learned that her name is mentioned in the list of "terrorists and extremists" of Rosfinmonitoring.

"FSB representatives sent a guidance to the Crimean post offices, which states that all money orders or correspondence received to my postal address must first be checked by the FSB, and then delivered to the recipient. Now, if my parents make an online order, it arrives in torn packaging. That means that FSB representatives monitor everything that comes to us, even if not addressed to me," says the journalist.

Since Anna Andrievska was staying in Kyiv, it was collectively decided not to engage in the fraudulent case so as not to help the FSB to "investigate" it. However, all the reporters of the Center for Investigative Reporting, which have remained in Crimea, had to experience FSB interrogations and searches.

"The court judgment did not indicate my status. The question arises: in what capacity was I searched? further recalls Natalia Kokorina. The investigator, who started a search in my room without me, met me. She was accompanied by two ladies, the witnesses. There was also a man who was checking the computers, and my mom and dad.

The investigator conducted the search very carefully. She took the book off the shelf, looked through it, and put into place. There were no overturned cabinets or broken shelves as it often happened in such cases.

I came around eight in the morning. The search lasted until around one p.m. It took her another hour and a half to fill in the documents. They took my parents' laptops, as well as my personal laptop I was keeping in my parents' apartment. They took some old documents dated 2012 or 2013, statements of works performed for the Center for Investigative Reporting. They also took away my business card.

During the search, I demanded counsel. At that moment, my colleague Serhiy Mokrushyn, whom I phoned on the way to my parents' apartment, was standing at the door. My colleagues, who learned about the search, invited counsel Dzhemil Temishev, who also was there with him. But I did not know that he was there.

All Ukraine knew about the search at my apartment; this was reported in all news releases. Mokrushyn transferred the information.

However, they did not provide me counsel. The investigator insisted that they had a right not to allow counsel when the investigating actions had already begun. I argued with her for a long time, but could do nothing, although the counsel called by my colleagues was standing at the door.

Upon completion of the search, the investigator said, "Now let's go for interrogation." I asked, "In what capacity?" "As a witness," she said. "Now as a witness." I asked, "What do you mean "now"?" "Well, you know, things can change. It's not difficult."

It means that they have exerted psychological pressure on me. They also pressed my parents. They were frightened for me. I was frightened myself, although I knew that it would happen one day. I know what I was going for when I decided to work in Crimea.

I had no choice whether to go or not to go to the FSB for interrogation. They are in my house, and I have to go. But I asked for a summons. Then the investigator said, "Why do you want a summons? You are unemployed. You do not need to justify your call for interrogation to your employer." In short, I literally stamped out the summons from them. They gave it to me at my insistence, when I came to them.

Before leaving I said, "I want a counsel. I will not go without him." She insisted that I did not need counsel because „we are going just to talk." They did not let me to call. Again, because of my persistence, she promised to call counsel herself.

On the way to the FSB, the investigator tells me that the counsel I requested would not be able to come. I said that I would not give testimony without a counsel. She again told me that I was still a witness, but everything could change if I quarrel with them.

I left to see counsel Dzhemil Temishev, who went from my parents' apartment to the FSB since he realized that they would bring me there. I say that I want him to be my counsel. The investigator denied gently. However, in the end he went with me. I was giving testimony with the counsel.

"I realized that if I leave Crimea, I won't be able to go back. I also understood that if stay, I won't be able to keep silent. This could end me up in prison."

The interrogation lasted more than six hours. They were asking what I was doing at the Center for Investigative Reporting? Why did I adhere to the pro-Ukrainian position? Why, with such a position, I had not left Crimea? What were my plans? They also asked me about the editor's office.

It was pretty nervous, with psychological pressure and intimidation, stories about how my work and my position could affect the lives of my relatives. The investigator asked why the journalists were waiting for her? How did they know about the search? She argued about the wording, I would say some words, and she wrote down others, thus changing the meaning of what I said. I forced her to rewrite the report and change the wording. She re-wrote the report several times.

After the interrogation, I went home. I had time to think what to do next. I began to feel that life was passing by, and I could change nothing. It was a short period of depression. Misunderstanding of what to do, where to go.

I realized that if I leave Crimea, I won't be able to go back. I also understood that if stay, I won't be able to keep silent. This could end me up in prison. I had to choose where it would make more sense for me to be. In June 2015, I finally packed up and left.

Between the search and June, I felt people watching me. I knew that my phones were intercepted. These people knew everything about me. This is also the pressure under which it is very difficult to live long. It is possible to endure some time, but not long.

On my first day in Kyiv, I did not know where to go and what to do. I had money only to lease an apartment for a month. At that time, all those who have been with me for many years moved from Crimea. In Kyiv, I felt myself much more at home than recently in Crimea.

I continued to work at the Center for Investigative Reporting. Almost nothing has changed in my life except the location and a very important thing, I cannot come and hug my parents when I want.

In May this year, I left the Center for Investigative Reporting and started working at Hromadske Television. I do not feel that we have parted, because I know that we all, the Crimean journalists, are one family. Still, it was a hard decision.

I cannot do without journalism. I believe that I will work in Crimea again, when it would return to the bosom of Ukraine."

Anna Andrievska says that because of the criminal case instituted against her, she cannot go home and can no longer work in the media under her own name, since any publication about the situation in Crimea may result in reprisals against her family. In fact, they have also become hostages.

Anna Andrievska. Photo by Krym.Realii (RFE/RL).

"Those who created this criminal case are great cynics. The authoritative international institutions have been declaring that Crimea is Ukraine for years. The authorities of the EU and Western countries introduced sanctions against Russia because of non-recognition of the Russian status of the peninsula. Still, there is no known criminal case, which would be instituted by the Russian authorities, for example, against some European or Western politicians. Instead, they work their frustration off on those whom they can reach, the Crimean people, on which they can press through the closest people," says Anna Andrievska.

> "The first blows on their side occurred after they learned that we are working at the Center for Investigative Reporting. They treated the journalists, especially the ones like our media, with particular ferocity."

The journalist of the Center for Investigative Reporting **Serhiy Mokrushyn**, who helped Natalia Kokorina with counsel, was not going to travel anywhere initially either. However, ultimately he had to do it. He says that he experienced the changes that have occurred after the occupation of Crimea by Russia.

Serhiy Mokrushyn, in 2014 correspondent of Center for Investigative Reporting in Simferopol. Photo by Stanislav Yurchenko (RFE/RL).

*"It was not closely related to the work, says Serhiy Mokrushyn. On June 2, 2014, my friend, director **Vladlen Melnikov** and I sang an offensive song about Putin in the street. The same one composed by the Kharkiv football fans. It was next to the central Lenin Square.*

We immediately felt that Russia has come. Under Ukraine, we could sing as much as we want and whatever we want, be it the President or someone else. And here we were caught by the "self-defense." The first blows on their side occurred after they learned that we were working at the Center for Investigative Reporting. They treated the journalists, especially the ones like our media, with particular ferocity.

We were interrogated at the headquarters of the "Crimean self-defense" at 26 Kirova Street, and beaten. The interrogation was led not by random people, but a member of the Public Council at the Council of Ministers of Crimea Aleksandr Yuriev and the member of the Simferopol City Council Anatoliy Petrov, ex-representatives of the Ukrainian authorities in Crimea, who have changed colors. Apparently, then they started looking for saboteurs and decided that saboteurs cannot help singing the anti-Putin songs on the streets. This was until we managed to write a SMS to Valentyna Samar, the leader of our center."

Valentyna Samar called the chief of staff of the "self-defense of Crimea" Dmytro Prostakov, whom she knew personally for many years. He worked as a security guard of the former speaker of the Crimean parliament and the leader of the Crimean Communists Leonid Grach.

"Prostakov explained, says Valentyna Samar, that the journalists were detained because they reproached the honor and dignity of the President of Russia. At my request to explain how exactly they did it he refused to speak. He also refused to release the staff of the Center for Investigative Reporting until the circumstances were clarified.

Counselor Serhiy Fomin and I came to the "self-defense headquarters" at Kirova Street, the wrestled office of the Republican Committee of the Communist Party of Ukraine. The counsel tried to enter, but the militants did not let him in. We called the police, a crew of the seconded Russians arrived, and after a while they brought Mokrushyn and Melnikov out.

The guys said they were beaten during the so-called "interrogation" and that they did not feel well, particularly Vladlen, who was beaten against the wall of plexiglass. He had blood and bruises on his head. The counsel and the advocate insisted that the police crew took Melnikov and Mokrushyn to the hospital. That evening Serhiy wrote a statement to the police about illegal detention and beating, but received no response."

Mokrushyn considers it fortunate that they were able to send an SMS, since he does not know how the situation would develop further.

"Then there were many missing and killed persons, says Mokrushyn. If not Valentyna, I don't know my future destiny, and whether I could recall it now.

Until I was hit pretty painfully in my head, I did not realize that suddenly everything has become prohibited. You cannot say what you think, and you cannot do what you want to do. This is how I was learning the new realities of Crimea.

Two days before my departure, I came as a journalist for the search of Oleksandr Kostenko, the Crimean Euro Maidan activist, against whom a criminal case was instituted; then he was condemned in Crimea. Kostenko's home was searched, and counsel Dmitriy Sotnikov saw that the FSB came for a search with their own witnesses. He asked me to be the witness during this search. I let the cameraman and the driver go and agreed.

My presence interfered with the FSB officers' work. They let me understand that they knew who I was, where I worked, the other facts, and hinted that I would have problems.

The next day, they searched my colleague Natalia Kokorina. After a whole day near her home, and then near the Crimean FSB, I realized that I might be next. So the next morning I went."

Today Serhiy Mokrushyn works in Kyiv as a master of programs of the Radio Liberty project Krym. Realii.

Russian unwittingly

The editor in chief of the BlackSeaNews, Crimean News Agency, **Andriy Klymenko** can be put in jail for five years in Russia for expressing the considerations which the Russian government in the Kremlin does not like. Fortunately, the journalist is in Kyiv.

"The criminal case against me was instituted as against a citizen of the Russian Federation, he says. It was one of the peaks of the legal arbitrariness of the occupation authorities, since I never got and was not going to get a Russian passport; we all, the residents of Crimea, were assigned the nationality of the occupying country automatically. I would laugh at this idiotic fact, unless it was so sad.

When I heard this, I immediately remembered how the Americans were amazed at the fact that the people can be forced to become Russian citizens. This is what I said in my report "Human Rights Abuses in Russian-occupied Crimea", which was published on the website of Freedom House on March 5, 2015.[16] And on March 6, I gave a speech on the same subject in the Atlantic Council in Washington.

> "The criminal case against me was instituted as against a citizen of the Russian Federation. It was one of the peaks of the legal arbitrariness of occupation authorities, since I never got and was not going to get a Russian passport."

Listeners simply could not believe that Crimea is back in times like Stalin's repressions in the Soviet Union of the 1930s. It is generally difficult to imagine such things to the civilized people in the 21st century. They

---

16   A. Klymenko. Human rights abuses in Russian-occupied Crimea / The Atlantic Council of the United States and Freedom House, 2015. URL: https://freedomhouse.org/sites/default/files/CrimeaReport_FINAL.pdf

were stunned when I told them about the technology of mass forcing the residents of Crimea to obtain Russian citizenship.

People in the West, knowing that citizenship is a very complex legal institution, just cannot understand this. They think in terms of international law and human rights. And Russia is outside it.

The Russian FSB office in the "Republic of Crimea and Sevastopol" instituted a criminal case against me on March 10, 2015, that is five days after the publication of my report and four days after my speech. Given that I exposed the destruction of human rights by the occupation authorities on the peninsula, it cannot be ruled out that this case was retaliation for my activity in the US.

I learned about it in early April, when many of my colleagues in Crimea were subjected to searches in my case. To date, according to the incomplete data, I know of two searches and interrogation of over twenty of my friends in Yalta.

As one of the major videos, they use my interview to Hromadske Television on July 6, 2014, in which I outlined the basic approaches of the Crimea de-occupation strategy, including different types of blockades and sanctions etc. The transcript of this interview on our website has collected about 6.300 million views as of yet. This material is the bases for reports on my identification during the interrogations.

I was accused of resorting to "public calls to commit the acts aimed at violation of the territorial integrity of the Russian Federation using the media, including information and telecommunication networks (in particular, the Internet)". This is part 2 of Article 280.1 of the Criminal Code, which was adopted in December 2013 and took effect on May 9, 2014. If Russia eventually catches me, I can stay in prison for up to five years or be punished by correctional labor for up to four hundred eighty hours.

The logic of Russia, of course, comes to the absurd. Russia took Crimea away from Ukraine by flagrant violation of international law. This act was actually not recognized by any country in the world, except for a few marginal ones. However, we may not talk about how to restore legitimacy and return Crimea to Ukraine, because Russia can put you in jail for that.

They also suffer from the spy delusion. During a "conversation" with one of the individuals whose comment we published, he said, "How could you talk to BlackSeaNews? Don't you know that its editor in chief is an American spy?"

In addition, I am now on the "List of terrorists and extremists (current);" as of December 21, 2017, my number is 3685. My number is growing continuously, as the list is being updated.

The state, which destroyed one hundred and fifty thousand of its own civilians during the "Chechen war", which attacked the sovereign state of Georgia and tore two chunks of its territory away, which began the war in Ukraine, dares to call someone a „terrorist."

Andriy Klymenko works in partnership with his colleague, **Tetiana Huchakova**. In 2000-2002, they were the reporters of the Ukrainian *Business* weekly in Crimea, and from 2005 to 2010, they were founders and editors of the *Bolshaya Yalta News* printed edition. Then they founded the BlackSeaNews news agency.

Tetiana Huchakova worked as an editor of the BlackSeaNews news feeds during the occupation. She was not going to leave Crimea, since she had a mother, who was 87 years old at that time. It was physically very difficult for the elderly woman to move somewhere. However, on April 9, 2015, the people with a search warrant came to her house in Yalta.

> "They were armed. It seemed that this crowd came to capture a gangster nest. Meanwhile, there was just me, my mother and son with a daughter in law in the house, who came from Kyiv to visit my mother and me."

"They came at seven, at the beginning of eight a.m., says Tetiana Huchakova. Usually, I am already working on the computer at seven. But that day I slept a little bit longer and, fortunately, had not opened the laptop. I would probably not have time to turn it off so that they did not see that I was working on it making news.

They went in very quickly. We have a private house in Yalta. I heard my mother chatting with someone. Lots of noise. Dogs barking. I went out and saw that the whole lane was full of cars, there are many people at the gate, and two are already in the yard. They say, "FSB. Open!"

I make a step back from the gate to take the key, come back and see that there were even more of them. One of them pulled a ski mask on his face. They were armed. It seemed that this crowd came to capture a gangster nest. Meanwhile, there was just me, my mother and son with a daughter in law in the house, who came from Kyiv to visit my mother and me.

Among those who participated in the search, there were former SBU agents, the traitors who broke the oath and changed colors. They were carrying a court order to search in a criminal case of Andriy Klymenko. I was indicated there as a witness.

The first question that I put was "I am a witness, and you conduct a search at my place. What would that mean?" They explained that this is done in cases where there is a suspicion that the witness can hide important documents.

They have been searching for ten hours. Our house area is a hundred square meters. We have a huge library, so it took them a lot of time to search for "secrets" among books. Since my son and his wife were staying there, we could keep control of the search and prevent them from throwing something.

I told them that we should see everyone, so that they did not pretend to find some white powder. They answered, "You are trying to justify yourself in advance?" "I'm not." "I just warn you." Eventually, they have not found any damaging material.

I was ready for them to come to me. I did not keep anything that could be of interest to the FSB at home. I had been instructed by people who knew what to do in such a situation. I had a right to a call, so I called these people on the pretext of finding counsel. They transferred the information to Kyiv.

In Kyiv, the people knew that they should fill the website with anything just to update it. That would show that it works without me.

My job as an editor was not prohibited by law. However, it did not matter for the occupation authorities. When they had something to complain about, they would have done it. Incidentally, during the search, they repeatedly watched whether the website was updated.

The search was conducted in two places simultaneously, in the house where I actually lived, and in an apartment that belongs to me and where my ex-husband lived. The investigators seized all media, phones and laptops.

In the evening, I was taken to the Yalta FSB for interrogation. The investigator tried to pretend friendliness. The questions were about the staff. The main question was about Andriy Klymenko. Did I read his post? What I think of it, do I share his views? The conversation lasted for at least an hour."

BlackSeaNews employees believe that they attracted the attention of Russian special services by publishing accurate information about how the annexation of the peninsula is taking place. The editor's office of the BlackSeaNews published a lot of material on the blocking of the Armed Forces of Ukraine and ships of the Naval Forces of Ukraine by Russian military units.

"A few days before the seizure of government buildings in Simferopol, says Tetiana Huchakova, *I suddenly received a call from a Russian news agency (I have wondered how they got my phone number) and asked whether it was true that many paratroopers had arrived in Yalta. There was no paratrooper at that time yet. This fact and subsequent events have shown that Russian journalists were informed about the annexation in advance.*

A day or two after this call, on February 25, two days before the seizure of the government buildings in Simferopol, we published a video of the Russian troops driving to the territory of the Russian Black Sea Fleet. It was evident that they were armed.

When the video appeared on our website, the people wrote reviews saying "don't force the situation, this is territory controlled by the Russians." Already then, we understood that something was being prepared, since the resort is not a base. It is intended for treatment and recreation. And those people came with weapons.

However, such comments of the readers can be understood. There was a strong pro-Russian sentiment in Crimea. But few could believe that the "brotherly people," as they called themselves, are able to treat their neighbor in such a way.

Then we were keeping track of the criminal actions of the Russian military, including the blockade of the Ukrainian military units. We were doing it regularly, and it could not help attracting the FSB attention."

Andriy Klymenko claims that after the illegal annexation of the peninsula, the BlackSeaNews website has become a source of reliable information about the situation in Crimea and violations of international sanctions.

He adds that since the occupation began, he had been working at a safe house. For security reasons, Klymenko moved to another apartment, about which only the most trusted people knew.

"The main reason for such secrecy was, says Andriy, that since the first days of the occupation we have quickly established a network of freelance reporters in garrisons of the Naval Forces of Ukraine blocked by Russian troops. Blackseanews is largely a maritime publication, so what kind of Black Sea news is possible without the sea? Therefore, we have always had friendly relations with the Ukrainian seamen.

In those dramatic days, we have become one of the few online resources giving hot information on Crimea. We saw that the people read us; the website traffic has exceeded 100,000 unique visitors per day. As journalists, we understood that we were doing an extremely important job. During that month, besides all other things, I had to give more than two hundred interviews and comments to Ukrainian and foreign mass media from the US, Canada, and almost all European countries from Spain to Norway. The only thing that I never did is talk on Skype, so that they could not decode my whereabouts.

We realized that in the chaos of those days, the special services of Russia will not start chasing us right away. However, at the end of March, just when the Ukrainian sailors left Crimea, we were informed that the Russian forces will come to our hiding place soon. Then it was decided to go to the mainland. The entire editor's office left Crimea, except for Tetiana Huchakova, who could not go at first because of her elderly mother. All of them are the people of Crimea, the residents of Yalta. Although, the majority of them are Russians by ethnic origin, but they did not want Putin to save them from the mythical "ferocity of the Ukrainian nationalists."

On April 6, 2014, I went from Crimea to Kyiv, and since then I have been living in the capital. Much of the editor's office followed me.

I brought all my family members from Crimea to the mainland of Ukraine. Currently, I have no relative in Crimea."

Tetiana Huchakova had to flee, too.

"After the search and first interrogation, several more interrogations were held between April and October 2015, says the journalist. In particular, they studied the business cards removed from me and asked about each of them, what kind of a person it was. During the last interrogation, on October 27, they played back the record of my telephone conversations and inquired what literally every phrase meant.

The mood of the Russian investigators has changed at the last inter-rogation significantly. She did not speak to me as to a possible source of information, but as an enemy to be exposed.

Then I felt that my status as a witness could be changed to a suspect. I managed to persuade my mother, and we left quickly. I crossed the ad-ministrative border on November 1, 2015.

Two windows were opened at the passport control point. I found the face that seemed more human to me, and went there. My mother went with me. I was trying not to show my excitement in all ways possible, but my mother could not stand it, she was taken bad at the window.

I told the border guard, "You see, the old lady is ill. Can I go to the car?" He allowed. I took her to the car. Mom said, "I was so afraid that you will not be released."

Protests in Crimea are dangerous. Police is arresting protesters.
Photo by Stanislav Yurchenko (RFE/RL)

On the neutral territory, my son and daughter in law have met us in the car. There I sighed with relief. Still, I was reflecting on the humiliating situation in which we found ourselves. I am the resident of Crimea. I was born and raised there. Suddenly invaders from another country came and established their own orders. These orders are contrary to the common sense and international law. I had to flee away from my own home because of invaders, because they could punish me for violation of their barbarous prescriptions."

Currently, the BlackSeaNews agency operates in Kyiv. Some of its staff settled in other cities of Ukraine. In addition to the information work, BlackSeaNews deals with monitoring and analytical activities.

"I was not informed about the criminal proceedings officially, says Andriy Klymenko. This information was not in the press or on websites in the public domain. Rather, it appeared from my words after I learned about it from colleagues.

The criminal proceedings against me means that my personal data and information are entered into the computer database of all power structures of Russia, namely the FSB, Border Guard Service, Ministry of Interior, customs etc. So if I appear in the territory of the Russia-controlled Crimea, in Russia, in the territory of Russian diplomatic missions outside of the RF, on marine vessels and other facilities of RF enjoying the extraterritoriality rights, I will arrested immediately.

It means that for me, visiting the occupied Crimea and Russian territory amounts to arrest, subsequent trial and imprisonment of up to five years. Also, I guess that Russia put me in the international wanted list, for example, in the countries of the Eurasian Union, such as Belarus, Armenia, Kazakhstan and others.

Therefore, I cannot, for example, go to Crimea to the graves of my parents."

Crimea Is Not for the Crimean Tatars

ATR is not for sale

Crimean Tatar ATR Channel currently broadcasts from Kyiv. The owner, management and journalists of the channel after the so-called "referendum" on the status of Crimea were trying to find a compromise with the new government without giving up their professional principles. The channel owner, businessman **Lenur Isliamov**, even went to work in the Russia-established "government" of Crimea for some time. However, no compromise with the occupiers could be reached, so the channel was forced to leave Simferopol.

The author of these lines firmly remembered a scene near the ATR channel. It was evening. The channel editor, I cannot remember his name, took me by the sleeve of my jacket, started pulling me and speaking with despair in his voice, *"Why do you leave us? Do not leave us!"* This man about fifty years old had tears in his eyes. Saying "you", he meant Ukraine, which was unable to secure the resistance to the aggressor at that time. This occurred on February 28 or March 1, 2014.

The Crimean Tatars, perhaps, more than others realized the consequences of what happened in those days. They experienced a mass deportation carried out by the Communist government of the Soviet Union in the middle of the last century. With great efforts, the Crimean Tatars have returned from exile to their homeland, and suddenly Russia came again, declared itself the successor of the USSR, and conducted military aggression against Ukraine.

The Crimean Tatars massively opposed the occupation. In the process of the peninsula annexation, they repeatedly went to mass protests against Russia's invasion of Crimea.

In those days, I was in the air of the ATR program led by the journalist **Zair Akadyrov** once or twice. Despite the working environment, the channel was dominated by concern, since Russian troops were moving from time to time by the building on the outskirts of the city, where the TV channel was hosted.

The then general director of the channel **Elzara Isliamova** says that they received information about a possible attack by the Russian military.

"We believed in it, because our journalists were covering the events round the clock live, showing what was happening actually, which could not be tolerated by those who seized Crimea, recalls Elzara Isliamova. We "issued a call"; and five to six hundred Crimean Tatars came to the TV channel. They were sleeping near the television channel building, two hundred people at once. It was scary, because our guards had sticks only. What could they do against an armed military?

We installed cameras to monitor what was happening outside of our building, and broadcasted that at night. The viewers told us that they did not turn off the TV set at night to watch whether an attack occurred. Fortunately, the military did not come.

An official close to the Russia-appointed head of government, Aksionov, said that he persuaded them not to do that. However, I think that the main factor was the presence of several hundred people in front of the channel. If the Russians tried to stop it, they could spill the blood of innocent people, and the Russians were aware of this at that time."

> "The guys with the cameras came closer to the entrance, and then a light noise grenade burst out between the first and the second front door. This is how they were scaring the journalists."

The then ATR reporter, **Shevket Namatullaev**, who is now working as a presenter of this TV channel in Kyiv, recalls that on the first day after seizure of the government buildings in Simferopol, the Russians demonstrated contempt for the journalists, and showed that they would only work with proven Russian media.

"When I approached the Verkhovna Rada at about eight in the morning, recalls Namatullaev, the pro-Russian activist, a local theater artist, was appealing to the journalists. For me, it was a specifically trained person who had to tell that there are people with super-arms inside, so that no one had the idea to storm the parliament.

He said that after meetings at night, the barricades were built from the flower beds and pallets, and at four in the morning two trucks with people in uniform and with weapons arrived. He said these were "our boys" who "came to help us." They helped them bring the ammunition; there were machine guns and the like.

The man said they were very friendly and willing to share every-thing. He invited the journalists to come to the Parliament. The glass on the front door was broken. I stopped aside, because my cameraman had not yet arrived at that time yet, and the guys with the cameras came closer to the entrance, and then a light noise grenade burst out between the first and the second front door. This is how they were scaring the journalists.

However, at the moment, we were not afraid too much, because we did not realize the whole scale of Russia's campaign for the annexation of Crimea. We could not imagine all the meanness towards dissent Crimeans which Russia is ready to resort to. Fear came after the Crimean Tatars began to disappear. However, it did not break our resolve.

When the Parliament session was held on the same day, only a Rus-sian channel managed to get there. They voted for the resignation of Ana-toliy Mohyliov, the head of the Ukrainian government in Crimea, and ap-pointment of the Russian puppet Serhiy Aksionov. According to our esti-mates, the Russians managed to collect only a little more than forty depu-ties, while the quorum required more than fifty.

Voting was held in violation of the law. That is why the journalists did not have access to the Parliament, because they could record this fact. It would be further evidence of Russia's illegal actions in the peninsula. No wonder, there is a lot of video since that time, and the video of the vote does not exist."

Shevket Namatullaev asserts that the pro-Russian activists contin-uously showed aggression towards ATR journalists. According to him, they were regularly accused of lies and corruption. The attacks occurred.

ATR reporter **Ibraim Umerov** and his cameraman were de-tained and lost their professional equipment.

"On March 15, we were broadcasting live the seizure of Bogdan-Auto showroom, recalls Ibraim. There were men with guns and masks. We came closer to them and began asking what happened. They said that some-one would come out later and explain. The Russian soldiers usually were silent, and these were talking. It seemed that this was not an army, but rather an armed group. We probably did not take particular note of it. Sub-sequent events have shown that we shouldn't have done so.

We were told to go to the other side of the road. Someone inside the office shouted to those who were outdoors to remove the camera. They ran to us, grabbed the cameraman, and then me. We tried to escape but failed.

They brought us to the office. The cameraman was first put to the floor. I also was ordered to lie down. I had no time to lie, because they raised the cameraman and started withdrawing all the media. They took away the camera, too.

When we were brought out, a man, the one who drove us away from the showroom first, came up. He started shouting that I had brass knuckles (which was not true). He hit me a couple of times. Then we were released."

Currently, Umerov leads the Crimean Tatar TV programs at UA/TV in Kyiv, broadcasting to foreign countries, and at the Ukrainian and Crimean Tatar radio Hayat.

The then ATR general producer Elzara Isliamova says that they had to make a lot of calls to find the captured equipment.

"Ultimately, we found out that it is kept by the so-called "self-defense", she says. We contacted their leaders and insisted that we were returned the camera. They did. I think that, even though they fought against journalists, still they were feared."

> "The press service manager comes up to me and asks me to get up. I say I would not get up because it is the anthem of the occupier."

Elzara Isliamova says that the channel was working under the slogan put forward by the civic activists of Ukraine, "A single country." It was placed as a backdrop in Ukrainian and Russian.

"We gave up cultural programs, says Ms. Isliamova, made hourly news, working in marathon mode, arranged live broadcasts with Ukrainian leaders, common talk shows with Ukrainian TV channels and Russian Dozhd, which was probably the only TV channel independent from the government. This lasted until April. We had been relatively untouched by then. And then they began to say that we need to change the channel policy, and adapt it to new realities."

Shevket Namatullaev believes that it was impossible to fit in the new realities. He had conflict with the latter-day Russians because of his irreconcilable attitude toward annexation.

"After annexation, I was accredited at the so-called "parliament," recalls Shevket, and I did not get up when the anthem was played before the start of the session.

The press service manager comes up to me and asks me to get up. I say I would not get up because it is the anthem of the occupier. Then everyone looked back at me. It happened about three times.

The then head of a parliament committee Yefim Fix wrote a letter to the TV channel management, which indicated that I might be punished for contempt of the state symbols. He suggested that the management conducted a conversation with me. I explained my position to the management. It grinned and said that I might consider that the conversation was conducted.

I agreed with the press service manager that for the period of the anthem I would be leaving the room. She agreed with this. However, it was a useless compromise, because soon they stopped accrediting us."

ATR reporter **Elvina Seitbullayeva** says that the appearance of the journalist with their channel logo immediately caused aggression by pro-Russian activists.

"I remember, there were rumors that the coupons for products would be introduced, she recalls. We went to ask people whether they think that was true and how they treated it. Three or four armed men approached the cameraman and me. One of them grabbed my hand. I asked, "Are you, such a big man, going to fight with me?" We were lucky then.

However, the cases where the pro-Russian activists prevented our work were numerous. They treated the Crimean Tatars as enemies. This attitude could be encountered not only by journalists, but also by any other representative of our people."

> "For the new government, it was very important to gain the loyalty of the Crimean Tatars. And it would be a success if the ATR, which stood on a pro-Ukrainian position, suddenly became loyal to the occupation."

ATR owner, the Russian businessman and ethnic Crimean Tatar **Lenur Isliamov** says that the new government offered him to sell the TV channel, but he refused.

"I came from Moscow to Simferopol as soon as I learned about the seizure of the government buildings, he says. The whole tragedy occurred in my eyes. The employees of the Crimean branch of the SBU were summoned one day and told "Ukraine does not exist any longer." Almost all

security service staff accepted Russian citizenship and changed colors. The same happened with the police. The army delivered up Crimea without a single shot.

The only organized (I stress, organized!) pro-Ukrainian power in the peninsula were the Crimean Tatars, the Mejlis of the Crimean Tatar people. And ATR channel was one of the tools to support the Crimean Tatars.

For the new government, it was very important to gain the loyalty of the Crimean Tatars. And it would be a success if the ATR, which stood on a pro-Ukrainian position, suddenly became loyal to the occupation. Therefore, they were persuading me to sell the TV channel.

My loyalty was sought through Moscow. I had thirty-four dealers' centers. One day, an excavator came to my office, dug a trench and blocked the entry and exit from my office. Then the Sanitary-Epidemiological Inspectorate came and began to raise the floor, looking for some unsanitary conditions. Then the fire inspectorate came, saying that the room does not comply with the fire safety regulations (however, this building was put into operation only five years ago and has operated without complaint). The tax service arrived and started the audit. The police arrived alleging that it had received a statement that we were keeping some explosives. They overtly tried to pull us to pieces.

At that time, I announced that I wanted to make the channel a joint stock company and let all Crimean Tatars buy shares, since if they destroy me as a businessman, it wouldn't be so easy for them to seize the TV channel from all Crimean Tatars as from me alone.

> "I felt that there was a task to bring the Crimean Tatar TV to Moscow on a platter."

Then, Serhiy Aksionov, the Kremlin trumpet to the Crimean government, offered me to meet. The meeting was attended by several people. He talked about me in the third person, a kind of disrespectful communication. He said he would give him, that is me, five or ten million, but the channel should not be anti-Russian. I said that the channel is not for sale. Thereafter, Aksionov said that I am „not capable of dealing with."

Then Dmytro Polonskyi, the „Minister of Information", Aksionov's deputy in their new „government", came to me to Moscow. He requested me to sell the channel, otherwise they would do the same one, and launch it on the same frequency, and no one would notice the substitution, so I should better sell it, since they would seize it anyway.

I said the same thing as the first time.

The people from the Ukrainian leaders, who fled after the Maidan, contacted me. In short, I felt that there was a task to bring the Crimean Tatar TV to Moscow on a platter.

Meanwhile, the assaults on my business did not cease. Once one of the employees of my bank said that she has a friend who can solve all problems. She told that the bank is bumped by the team of Oleg Belaventsev, who was Putin's representative in Crimea. She says "if you write a letter in his name that you agree to sell the TV channel or to transfer it to the management and make it loyal to the government..." However, as the best option, she suggested selling the channel to her. She said she has bought several radio stations in Crimea.

Logo of ATR TV channel.

In addition, she said an interesting thing that her husband was one of those who was "annexing" Crimea to Russia. He is military, the general. I realized that it was going about the Main Intelligence Agency.

I asked if I agreed to sell it, for whom would you register it? She called the name of a person close to Aksionov, his longtime business partner."

Lenur Isliamov realized that the Russian government is not going to weaken its pressure on the Crimean Tatars and only simulates loyalty after he was appointed as a "deputy prime minister" in Serhiy Aksionov's "government."

After the annexation, the Crimean Tatars decided to delegate two persons to the newly created Crimean government. Radio Liberty reported on April 1, 2014 that the Crimean Tatar Mejlis decided to consent to the entry of Lenur Isliamov (as the first deputy chairman of the "Council of Ministers"), who is also the owner of the ATR TV channel, and Mejlis deputy chairman, Zaur Smirnov, as the "Chairman of the National Committee on Nationalities and Deported Citizens", to the "Council of Ministers."

Also, Mejlis held that based on Isliamov's and Smirnov's performance, it would review the matter of the further participation of the Crimean Tatars in the work of the "Council of Ministers."

"They are not politicians. They addressed the issue of support of the Crimean Tatars, they will not bear any political burden. This burden rests with the Mejlis and Kurultai," as the head of the Crimean Tatar people Refat Chubarov commented on this Mejlis decision.

Mejlis also ordered its representatives in the "Crimean government" to submit a weekly report on the specific work of the Crimean Tatars support.

However, the leader of the Crimean Tatars Mustafa Dzhemilev spoke against such cooperation between Mejlis and separatist authorities in Crimea.

"I finally said to them, "You probably want to deport us all from Crimea!" When I said this after three hours of negotiations, everyone was silent."

"The murders, kidnappings and intimidation of the Crimean Tatars were ongoing then recalls Lenur Isliamov. I was tasked to stop it. To ensure that May 18, the anniversary of deportation of the Crimean Tatars by the USSR government, was celebrated properly. On the third day of my stay there, I realized that I would fail.

There was a meeting. It involved the then representative of the Russian President in Crimea Oleg Belaventsev, the head of the so-called "government" of Crimea Serhiy Aksionov and other officials. They as a group were trying to explain to me that the Crimean Tatars should not celebrate May 18, "Why are you trumpeting your Crimean Tatar nationality?" "Behave calmly, and everything will be okay." These were their questions and recommendations. They just did not understand why it was so important for us, why we resisted. Why we did not hang a Russian flag on the channel, although it would simplify the situation for us a lot.

The quarrel was stated at the table. I finally said to them, "You probably want to deport us all from Crimea!" When I said this after three hours of negotiations, everyone was silent. Then I realized that I had said something they all knew, that they wanted. Belaventsev adjourned the meeting right away.

Then Belaventsev initiated another meeting involving the Crimean Tatar Mejlis Chairman Refat Chubarov, his deputy Akhtem Chyigoz, and Mufti of the Crimean Muslims Emiraly Ablayev. Their side was represented by Belaventsev, Aksionov, head of the Crimean "office" of the FSB Viktor Palagin, "prosecutor" Natalia Poklonska designated by him, and Simferopol mayor Viktor Ageiev.

The question arose: what to do with May 18, the 70th anniversary of deportation of the Crimean Tatars outside Crimea?

Belaventsev said that we should better not celebrate it, because there are forces willing to destabilize the situation. Aksionov said he was bothered that his Russian people were hiding in their homes every year on this day, being afraid of the Crimean Tatars. Chubarov said that we would celebrate as we used to. Belaventsev said that he would decide. Chubarov denied that the Crimean Tatar people would decide. More tension was created.

Prohibiting the Crimean Tatars to celebrate their national tragedy is like forbidding the Ukrainians to mention the Famine and to Jews the Holocaust."

On May 18, 2014, there were crowds of police on the streets of Simferopol. Helicopters were flying above the city. Movement in the city center was completely blocked. For the first time in 25 years, the day of mourning was moved from the center to the suburbs. This is how the new government "celebrated" the 70th anniversary of the deportation of the Crimean Tatars. On that day, the so-called "Crimean self-defense" captured the former ATR reporter **Osman Pashayev** and his team.

Osman Pashayev. Photo by Krym (RFE/RL).Crimean Tatar journalist.

"Shortly before, I left the ATR and founded my project, Crimean Open Channel, tells **Osman Pashayev**. *I invested all my savings in it, and within a month, the Ukrainians transferred me around fifty thousand hryvnias. We tried to reach the places where the signs of Ukraine were remaining, as well as state bodies gradually seized by the invaders.*

On May 18, my team and I went to cover the mourning events dedicated to the anniversary of the deportation of the Crimean Tatars. At one p.m. Kyiv time, two p.m. Crimean time, we arrived at Chekhov Street. The movement was blocked there.

We managed to record one interview. We wanted to move towards Lenin Square. We were attacked by nine men. Two of them were in civilian clothes, seven in camouflage. "Show your authorization to shoot at the Council of Ministers!" they requested strictly.

We showed our identity cards. Then they snatched the camera with a tripod, tablets, and pulled a backpack with our belongings. They took us to 26 Kirova Street. There used to be the office of the Communist Party, later turned into the headquarters of the so-called "self-defense" of Crimea.

We were stuffed to the second floor, ordered us to face the wall, leaning our hands against the wall, feet shoulder-width apart. When we put our feet closer, they beat us on the legs, making us place them wider. They started beating me after I asked if we were detained and whether there was a detention report. They gave an affirmative answer to the first question.

Four hours later, cameraman **Cengiz Kyzhyn**, *a Turkish national, and I were taken to the Central Police Department at 20 Futbolistiv Street.*

We were taken to one office or another. Ultimately, I gave my witness to the representative of the Investigative Committee of Russia Viktor Shchukin. It turned out that I was questioned as a witness in the murder of a Berkut fighter on the Maidan. It looked as if not several dozen of people were murdered on the Independence Square, but only one Berkut officer.

While I was staying at the headquarters of the "self-defense", all my equipment went missing, a laptop, three routers, one ours and two provided by Hromadske Television. My phone was gone. They seized $100 of 250 and UAH 500 of 900 from my purse."

On May 18, 2014, the occupation authorities controlled the rally of Crimean Tatars on helicopters. Photo by Stanislav Yurchenko (RFE/RL)

According to Pashayev, five more journalists were detained there.

Osman Pashayev does not come to Crimea any more. He worked for some time at ATR channel in Kyiv. Now he is the executive producer of UA: Krym creative association of Public Broadcasting.

Ten days after the anniversary of the deportation of the Crimean Tatars, on May 28, 2014, ATR owner Lenur Isliamov was dismissed from office of the Deputy Chairman of the so-called "Council of State" of Crimea.

"Literally the FSB landing burst into the channel. They came to search us in masks with guns. A gunman was standing in each room and prohibited people to move."

"Unfortunately, in my opinion, Mr. Isliamov is quite politically engaged in his work. So we decided that we need to have a less prejudiced person in this position," said on this occasion the deputy chairman of the "State Council" of the Crimea Grygoriy Ioffe to the reporters, adding that Isliamov was engaged by Mejlis political structure. He was cited[17] by RIA Novosti.

"In recent days, I did not even go to work, says Isliamov, because it made no sense. Work in the government revealed that no agreement with the occupiers could be reached at all. The only policy they can understand and use is orders from the top to be performed by everyone."

Elzara Isliamova argues that the channel policy did not change.

"ATR continued highlighting the issues. We showed the searches conducted in Crimea, and talked about the political persecutions. No channel talked about it, only ours, says Isliamova, and this was very annoying to the new government. It needed loyalty.

In January 2015, literally the FSB landing burst into the channel. They came to search us in masks with guns. A gunman was standing in each room and prohibited people to move. Editor in chief Lilia Budzhurova went live and reported it. It turned out they were searching for our records from the meetings of the Crimean Tatars near the Verkhovna Rada of Crimea on February 26, 2014. They used to send the requests to us, and we sent them our stories that were in the air. However, they wanted the archives.

In this way, they were seeking the rally participants to condemn them. At that time, Crimea was controlled by Ukraine. They did not care of it, anyway. They judged the protesters by Russian legislation, which is a legal absurdity.

---

17   Public Council of the Crimea: Ysliamov removed from office because of engagement / RIA Novosti, 28.05.2014. URL: https://ria.ru/world/20140528/10096 87527.html

Elzara Isliamova. In 2014 general director of the Crimean Tatar ATR TV channel. She is still in Crimea. Photo is from her archive.

Another possible reason for the search was that the new government was going to launch a Crimean Tara Millet channel loyal to it, and they needed our archives. However, we secured ourselves, and they found nothing.

Then they delayed the issue of a license to us. According to the Russian laws, the media had to re-register and obtain a license for broadcasting. The Crimean media had to do it by April 1, 2015. We submitted the documents four times, and received four refusals because of a wrong letter or a wrong comma place. And once we were asked to prove that the owner is an adult. Clearly, they were deliberately looking for an excuse to refuse the license issue.

We were negotiating, since we understood the importance of the Crimean Tatar channel in Crimea. We even were willing to abandon the policy at all, and remain a purely culture channel. However, in the sidelines, they told us openly that it was a political decision.

I see four reasons why they treated us in such a way:

First, the owner refused to sell the TV channel, to transfer it under their control. Hence, there was no guarantee of the channel loyalty to power.

Secondly, they did not forgive us that we covered the February 26 events online, showing what was actually happening in Crimea. The world's largest media included our materials in their reports. The UN and the European Commission use our materials; they could be evidence in the international court on the accusation of Russia. It was annoying to the authorities.

Third, even under the new conditions, we adapted and still were following our professional standards, telling the truth about the current problems of searches and persecution. Now is can be shown, perhaps by the all-Russian NTV, but under a specific perspective distorting the situation.

Fourth, the Crimean Tatar channel is a channel of the minority, which came first in the ratings, even ahead of the Ukrainian ones. Twenty-five to thirty percent of our viewers were Crimean Tatars, while the others were other nationalities. In Russia, this could not be so by definition. Its

national channels are stuck in the 90's of the last century in terms of quality. Therefore, it is simply impossible to allow the presence of a high-quality national channel in Russia.

We had no other choice. Under the Russian laws, if the media is undocumented, it not only has to pay a fine, but also is liable to equipment seizure. And a criminal case shall be instituted against its director.

ATR was forced to stop broadcasting in Crimea. The inscription says that 0 days 00:00:00 left to the end of the broadcast.

The day before the closing, on March 30, 2015, they made a last attempt to outbid us. We were invited by the so-called "minister of information"

Dmytro Polonskyi and asked about the conditions under which we as the whole team would agree to serve them. We refused.

On the eve of April 1, we announced an open day. Our audience came to say goodbye to us. It was very sad that we failed to keep the channel in Crimea."

Many from the ATR channel stayed on the peninsula due to various circumstances, including the former director general Elzara Isliamova.

"We organized the production, and called it Qaradeni production (Black Sea production), says Isliamova. We deal with cultural projects, and launched an online portal Crimeantatars.club, dedicated to Crimea and Crimean Tatars. We organized a children's talent show Dzhanly ses (live voice), a humorous project K'yrymda Yasha (live in Crimea). We also shot the video sequences for the Crimean Tatar songs, sketches, and this summer we shot a children's film "Hıdır dida" (grandfather Hıdır).

I think that the government does not bother us and lets us work because we deal with cultural projects only. Albeit we have more than 50,000 subscribers, we do not have a TV channel."

ATR television channel resumed broadcasting in Kyiv on June 18, 2015.

Journalist Elvina Seitbullayeva, who is currently working in Kyiv, recalls that on February 26, 2014, after a big rally involving the Crimean Tatars, she was approached by a man, *"He gave me a stone wrapped in a white cloth. He said, "Take it to the memory of this day." I asked why. He said that today was a historic day and tomorrow things could change. Huge changes were coming. I took the stone. The next day, when I learned of the capture of the parliament and government, I recalled the man and his stone. I kept the stone."*

Elvina cannot get home because she has been covering the Russian aggression in eastern Ukraine for a year. She is afraid that she could have troubles with the FSB because of this fact. However, she believes that she would return to Crimea and find that stone.

Notice: entry denied

On August 10, 2014, at about seven thirty a.m., a citizen of Turkey **İsmet Yüksel**, who had lived in Crimea for about 20 years with his family, during entry to Crimea from the mainland of Ukraine, had received a notice from the Russian border guards that his entry to Crimea and the Russian Federation is denied for five years. Ismet was the general coordinator of the Krymski Novyny News Agency (QHA). His wife **Gayana Yüksel** served as the editor in chief of this agency established in 2005.

On August 12, during a press conference in Simferopol, the so-called "prime minister" of Crimea Serhiy Aksionov answered the following to the question why İsmet Yüksel was denied entry,[18] *"All individuals breaking the inter-ethnic peace in Crimea will be denied entry to the territory of the republic. All the people who are splitting the Republic of Crimea on ethnic grounds and are reasonably suspected of such actions will be subjected to administrative measures in accordance with the laws of the Russian Federation. In relation to such persons, the most stringent measures will be applied in order to preserve peace and calm in the republic."*

Aksionov did not refer to the article of the law, under which it was decided to deny entry, and did not call the institution which has made such a decision. Meanwhile, the decision to deny the entry of İsmet Yüksel to Crimea, as was reported to the Yüksels, was adopted in Moscow by FSB headquarters, whereby İsmet Yüksel was declared a person "threatening the territorial integrity of the Russian Federation."

Gayana Yüksel insists that Aksionov's words in response to the question about her husband again demonstrate the incompetence of the Crimean puppet head and are a part of a campaign to discredit the Crimean Tatars.

"The Crimean Tatars overwhelmingly disagreed with the Crimea annexation, she said, and wanted the peninsula to remain as a part of Ukraine. Therefore, appointed officials on instructions from Moscow primarily started with fighting the indigenous people of Crimea as a hostile force.

---

18   Aksionov: entry to the Crimea will be denied to anyone who is trying to kindle ethnic conflict / Krym. Realii, 12.08.2014.URL: https://ru.krymr.com/a/2652 6754.html

They began taking steps in order to squeeze the non-loyal Crimean Tatar media, including our agency, out of Crimea. The denial of entry to the agency founder is one of such steps."

The denied entry notice was served after İsmet, Gayana and their 14-year-old daughter Dzhanike, returning from Kyiv to Crimea on the night of 9 to 10 August by car, having waited for eight hours in a queue to the point of administrative control in Armiansk, the Crimean peninsula. Having produced their passports, the family was offered by the FSB Border Service employee to drive the car to the side without explanation.

On May 18, 2014, police are going to control the rally of the Crimean Tatars. Photo by Stanislav Yurchenko (RFE / RL)

İsmet Yüksel says that the guards did not know the reasons for the legal arbitrariness applied to them:

"After we produced our passports, he says, the Russian border guard left with all our documents. Having returning after some time with his colleague, he said that we need to drive our personal vehicle to the side and wait. The reasons for actual detention were not explained to us.

We had been waiting for an hour and a half. During this time, to our questions about the basis for detention, the border guard officers only reported that the check is pending, and an error might have occurred.

At about seven thirty a.m. the board guard (probably a lieutenant), who took our documents, returned them to me and my family members and said, that "the citizen of Turkey İsmet Yüksel is denied entry to the Russian Federation."

At the request to explain the reasons and the legal basis for such a denial, the official said that he did not know and could only provide the article number, the content of which we could read on the Internet.

Then we were approached by the Russian military without identification marks who said that the decision to deny entry was made by the FSB of Russia. He also said that he would like to help us and asked me to show my passport. He was asking what, in our opinion, could be the cause of the denial. Having seen a US visa in the passport, he asked what I was doing in the US. Then, together with my passport, he went in an unknown direction."

> "And then the soldier snatched the notice from Gayana's hands, saying that their business is only to inform me about the denial and he wouldn't give me the notice. It was an action, that does not fit into any civilized norm. We were shocked by such behavior."

10 minutes later, the same soldier, in a more aggressive mood, came to us with two sheets of A4 paper bearing several signatures of the Russian border guards and reading "NOTICE."

The document, drawn up in Russian, read that İsmet Yüksel, a citizen of Turkey, is denied entry to the territory Russian Federation until June 30, 2019 under article (we failed to remember its number). Should he violate this ban, he would be prosecuted in accordance with Art. 322 of the RF Criminal Code "Illegal crossing of the border of the Russian Federation" and further detailing the penalties for the said violation.

The notice text was read and translated by my wife. I did not sign the notice on the denial of entry to Russia due to the fact that I do not speak Russian and the Crimean Tatar translation was not provided. Consequently, I could not understand the content of the document, its legal implications and consequences of signing the same properly. My wife translated my words to the soldier.

At this very moment, our daughter began to cry, and my wife tried to calm her. And then the military man snatched the notice from Gayana's hands, saying that their business is only to inform me about the denial and he wouldn't give me the notice. It was an action, that does not fit into any civilized norm. We were shocked by such behavior.

> "The most striking point in the part where the FSB had to provide evidence that led to the entry denial, is that we were not informed. The case was classified as "secret"."

After this incident, we were approached by the border guards (presumably the lieutenant) and said that my family can go on (we were five in the car, me, my wife and daughter, the younger brother of my wife and his wife), but I have to leave. Saying that, he waved toward the Ukrainian checkpoint.

My daughter with my wife's brother and his wife went to Crimea to their family, and my wife and I had to return to Kyiv.

We filed claims on infringement of our right to enter, the right to travel, the right to live on our homeland and in our home to the courts in Crimea and Moscow. We have passed through all authorities in Russia. My case is currently before the European Court of Human Rights. The most striking point in the part where the FSB had to provide evidence that led to the entry denial, is that we were not informed. The case was classified as "secret." When the FSB employees were providing the data to the court, our representative was removed from trial. When we received the judgments, and we had three of them, neither operative nor narrative parts contained the reason for the entry denial.

I have lived in Crimea for 20 years, there is my house, where I resided with my family. I obtained a permit for permanent residence on the peninsula from the Ministry of Internal Affairs of Ukraine in Crimea. There I was engaged in social and professional activities, was the general coordinator of the QHA Krymski Novyny News Agency and advisor to the Chairman of Mejlis on relations with Turkey, as well as engaged in business.

The inability to get home in Crimea results in the disruption of my family and professional relationships, as well as serious moral and material damages. As a result of these illegal actions of the Border Service employees, my rights to freedom of movement and choice of the place of residence were violated."

Gayana Yüksel says her story and the story of her husband are an inexplicable consequence of the Russian occupation of Crimea and its struggle against the indigenous people Crimea.

"The beginning of the occupation for me was a shock, recalls Gayana. With all this range of feelings that accompany a state of shock, anxiety, insecurity, and the oppressive burden of feeling that we will reach the abyss. Despite all the difficulties that were in Crimea, we lived as a part of our state in Ukraine. I never thought that such illegal action is possible.

Therefore, the events of February 27, 2014, when military equipment began to arrive when the situation in Crimea was very tense, explosive, I perceived everything very tragically. By the way, I am not alone. Many of our compatriots experienced this shock. We received information from different corners over Crimea. The people were sitting on their suitcases, calling, asking the remove their children. They said, "We have nothing but children..."

We knew that in order to avoid provocations and attacks on the homes of Crimean Tatars in various parts of Crimea and towns of organized pickets of the Crimean Tatars. In the villages, the people slept in mosques not to remain in homes and avoid any provocation. Today, many people say that the seizure of Crimea was predictable. However, I think that for most civilians of Crimea this was unexpected.

The Crimean Tatars have had experience of persecution on ethnic grounds. Therefore, most of them were against the occupation. Some went to the rallies, someone experienced it in the family, someone personally. But most were against.

We were often asked, "Why do you care? You did not have statehood in the times Ukraine, and you have no statehood in the times of Russia. What did you lose? Why are you against the occupation?" The answer is very short. We have a very good genetic memory. We know what the empire did during the first annexation in 1783, when nearly three hundred thousand Tartars had to leave the peninsula. They parted to Romania, Bulgaria, Turkey, which at that time had the status of the Ottoman Empire.

We remember the Soviet deportation of the communist government in 1944. Our old people remember very well what is a soldier with a weapon coming into the house. They saw it as a child. They see it again, being elderly, having returned to Crimea after 50 years of deportation. They saw it in 2014.

I do not know how short-sighted should a person be not to under-stand that no development, no progress is expected for the Crimean Tatars in the environment created by the Russian state.

It turned out this way. We are shaking every day of horrible infor-mation coming from the peninsula. However, our people have learned to respond to challenges.

For example, the situation with Renat Paralamov, who was kid-napped and tortured. Law enforcement officers came to take him by car, and she, an ordinary Crimean woman, said "Follow him." Even she is aware that the law enforcement officers could not be trusted.

Nine cars followed him, but the road patrol blocked the road, and they failed to track the car. He was taken somewhere. The next day Renat was found beaten and tired, with broken legs. What is it? Are these the realities in which we live in the times of Ukraine? No! These are the realities brought by the aggressor state to the peninsula.

> "We have been frequent visitors to the FSB, the prosecutor's office. I was summoned to the Center to Combat Extremism, where the so-called "prophylactic conversations" were conducted or administrative protocols were prepared retroactively for operations in 2006 or 2009, that is, at the time when Crimea was controlled by Ukraine."

In February 2014, we decided for ourselves that we should stay in Crimea. After the so-called "referendum," I knew that our stay in Crimea will be very difficult and dangerous. Our information resource held to the pro-Ukrainian position in all these views. It was seen from the materials that we have published.

Gradually, the circle began to narrow; we have been frequent visitors to the FSB, the prosecutor's office. I was summoned to the Center to Com-bat Extremism, where the so-called "prophylactic conversations" were conducted or administrative protocols were prepared retroactively for op-erations in 2006 or 2009, that is, at the time when Crimea was controlled by Ukraine.

All our employees were under surveillance. Whatever public event we attended, the security officers always came up and recorded their pass-port details. Not to mention myself.

I would compare that situation with our activities in the Ukrainian Crimea. We started working in 2006. Then our compatriots noted that the news about the events in Crimea reach them in three or four days, or even in a week. Based on the need to ensure efficient delivery of information, we created his agency.

There were problems and issues to be addressed. However, all these were purely business issues. Most importantly, we could work freely. We had access to various sources of information, were able to participate in various activities, and had free access to all facilities.

We were deprived of it in May 2014, shortly after the illegal "referendum" on March 16. By the way, we published an article under the headline that the "referendum" held in Crimea not be recognized by the world, and in May we were "banned" and not allowed to attend any event at the state level.

We could not fully perform our duties to collect, process and disseminate information. For example, we could not get to the "Council of Ministers" of Crimea, to the Crimean parliament, which then was called "Gosudarstvennyi Sovet," and could not get through to many sources.

The "Council of Ministers" of Crimea responded to us with a false official letter that we do not have state accreditation. It was just a formal reply and manipulation, because at that time no Crimean media had Russian accreditation. The re-registration procedure had to be passed by December 1, 2014, and then was extended to April 1, 2015.

Only later we learned that secret directives were issued in respect of our agency and several pro-Ukrainian Crimean media not to allow us to various events, not to give us the opportunity to highlight them. So we felt the difference between Ukraine and Russia very quickly.

All this pressure and a ban on the residence of my husband in Crimea encouraged me to move to the mainland, since full-fledged work on the peninsula has become impossible.

After moving to mainland Ukraine, we, like the other Crimean media forced to leave the peninsula, are in very difficult conditions. Why? Because we talk about the language and the territory to which we do not have access. But we do not loose connection with Crimea.

Currently, the best way to contact Crimea is electronic media, so when we were asked to open a radio station, we agreed. Last year we participated in the competition of the National Council on Television and Radio Broadcasting of Ukraine for radio frequencies and were awarded frequency 103.5 FM in Kherson.

Not to say that it is very good, it is slightly away from the place where our target audience in the Kherson region lives, but we work, since it is the first step to develop our radio network and online broadcasting.

In addition to the frequency, we broadcast online and on the website of Krymski Novyny News Agency. Although we launched it just recently, we are watched and heard in Crimea. We hope that we will be able to expand our field of activity, because our work precipitates the return of Crimea." **Professional amateurs**

The phenomenon of civic journalism has emerged in Crimea

Forced to become a journalist.

In October 2022, Crimean Tatar Seyran Saliyev, his wife Mumine Saliyeva, their four kids—one boy and three girls, and the mother of the head of the family Zodiye Saliyeva –performed salah. At first glance there is nothing unusual in this. Joint prayers—salah—is a religious obligation for Muslims.

However, there was one peculiarity which distinguished this salah from those held in this and many other Muslim families: the last time this family had prayed together at home under normal circumstances was five years earlier on October 11, 2017. On the next day, at around four o'clock in the morning, FSB officers of the Russian Federation had broken into their apartment on the fifth floor of the apartment building in Bakhchysarai, near Sevastopol.

The FSB officers were armed with assault rifles, everyone was wearing masks, and there was a dog with them. They stormed into the bedroom. Seyran asked them to leave the room to give his wife a chance to get dressed. While Mumine was getting dressed in a hurry, her children were screaming in fright. As she came out of the bedroom, she saw that her husband was lying on the floor with his hands cuffed He raised his head, and she noticed a large bruise on his forehead.

Among the uninvited guests there was a man without a mask who was wearing a suit.

"I realized that it was the investigator", Mumine Saliyeva recalls. "I turned to him: 'What is going on here? I am the human rights defender; I will record all violations and will file a complaint. You are obliged to articulate on what grounds you knocked my husband to the ground and handcuffed him. He is not a suspect or an accused. You have no right to act this way.'" They uncuffed her husband. The investigator read the resolution on arraignment under the article "terrorism". "It was clear to me that it was a fabrication of the criminal case. They conducted a search. Nothing was found. However, my husband was taken outside and since then he hasn't returned to his home".

Seyran Saliyev, alongside with other seven Crimean Tatars—Marlen Asanov, Memet Belialov, Server Zakiryayev, Ernes Ametov, Timur Ibragimov, Edem Smailov, and Server Mustafayev—were conveyed to the Russian city of Rostov-On-Don. He was charged under articles 205.5 and 278 of the Criminal Code of the Russian Federation for membership of Hizb-ut-Tahrir, which the Russian Federation considers a terrorist organization, and with violent upheaval and power retention.

More than 78 court hearings were held. The trials lasted five years. The only evidence presented were audio recordings in mosques, in which members were discussing religious and political matters.

Seyran Saliyev was sentenced to 15 years in a maximum-security penal colony. Human rights defenders consider this case to be politically motivated.

Mumine Saliyeva is convinced that her husband was doomed to be politically persecuted after the two of them began covering the repressions against the Crimean Tatars in Crimea after the occupation in 2014.

Mumine has a typical biography for the Crimean Tatars. She was born in Tajikistan, where her forebears had been deported to from Crimea by the Soviet authorities in 1944. As the Soviet regime became somewhat liberalized under Mikhail Gorbachev coming to power in the mid-1980s, Crimean Tatars began to return to their ancestral homeland. Mumine's parents moved to the village of Aromatne in Bilogirsk district in the early 1990s.

She says that local children were hostile to the newcomers. She believes that the necessity to defend herself from harassment helped her develop a fighter's spirit. She graduated from school with a gold medal, then finished the Crimean Engineering Pedagogical University and currently she is working on a post-graduate degree and preparing to write her PhD thesis.

In September 2006 she married Seyran, a philologist. Since his early childhood he was accustomed to public activism: when Seyran was three years old, he accompanied his mother Zodiye to a picket in Moscow's Red Square, where protesters demanded permission for Crimean Tatars to return to Crimea. He took an active part in the public life of his city. In particular, he taught children Arabic and Turkish, and trained them in wrestling.

Before 2015, Mumine's interests focused on family and science. But after the occupation of the Peninsula, she, together with her husband, took an active part in protecting Crimean Tatars from repression from the occupying authorities.

On January 23, 2015, in the village Orlyne in Sevastopol district, four Crimean Tatars were arrested: Ruslan Zeytullayev, Rustem Vaitov, Nuri Primov and Ferat Sayfullayev.

During the searches, their wives' phones were also taken away, so they could not call them for support.

The Saliyev couple went to the trial. Those arrested were accused of membership of the organization Hizb-ut-Tahrir, which has been banned in the Russian Federation since 2003 and, after the occupation of Crimea, had been banned on the Peninsula as well. Non journalists were not allowed to film or record in court. Mumine wrote down the twists and turns of the trial process in her notebook. According to her words, the Crimean Tatars were tried for "kitchen talks".

The four defendants had been discussing the situation in Crimea and criticizing the occupation of the Peninsula.

Another man ingratiated himself with them, but secretly recorded their conversations on a Dictaphone and sent it to the investigating authorities. Mumine believes that he was a FSB decoy. At the trial he testified as a secret witness—only a recording of his altered voice was used. The defendants came to the conclusion that it was one of their acquaintances under the alias Adnan. The only basis for charges were the audio recordings; no other evidence was provided.

In the joint report of human rights organizations Euromaidan SOS, the Center for Civil Liberties and the "Open Dialogue" foundation under the name "28 hostages of the Kremlin", which was published in January 2016, the following was said about this case: *"It is important to note that in Ukraine the organization "Hizb-ut-Tahrir", which is engaged in religious, political and educational activities, operates without hindrance. According to the general ideas of Western democratic countries, given organization is not considered extremist. However, after the occupation of Crimea with the Russian Federation, the organization "Hizb-ut-Tahrir" became banned, and thousands of its supporters were under the threat of criminal prosecution".*

Mumine compiled her trial notes and posted it on Facebook. She believes that this was the exact time when her public activity as a civic journalist had begun.

The next report convinced her of the efficacy of journalism. Shortly after the trial of the four Crimean Tatars, the Saliyev couple decided to pay a visit to their families. They were shocked with what they saw at Ruslan Zeytullayev's home. Although he was building a house, his family didn't have enough funds. So they lived in a cheap rented apartment with a rotten floor, and from its cracks cockroaches and other insects crept out.

Ruslan's wife Meryem explained that there was underground water there, and therefore the humidity was very high. From behind her skirt, her three daughters were peeking with eyes full of fear. They were frightened by the arbitrariness of the Russian security forces and were afraid of strangers. The woman and three children were alone with such issues. Mumine described Meryem's story and posted the report on Facebook.

"A lot of people responded", she says, *"they began to help this family — some donated money, some agreed to work on the construction site. People helped to finish the construction of the house and the family could move there".*

Meryem Zeytullayeva recalls: *"Since my husband's arrest, the year has been very difficult for me. Trials, inmate packages, father's passing. If it wasn't for people's help, I don't know what would have happened to me and my children. Young guys, I didn't know them — every time those were different people, were finishing up our house. They put their soul into it, into every detail. When we moved there it is hard to explain what we felt. We cried with joy. Daughters were happy. It was warm, light and spacious. It is really way easier to overcome the problems in unity".*

Mumine Saliyeva says that at the beginning there were many people who thought that the arrests could not be groundless; as they say, there is no smoke without fire. This was why she had to clarify in her publications that in fact this was political repression, an attempt to muzzle Crimean Tatars, an attempt to force them to stay quiet.

"I did not intend to be a journalist" Mumine says. *"However, the new government took measures and there were no professional journalists left, who were not under their control. Someone had to do it. Construction workers, teachers, entrepreneurs turned into civic journalists. Everyone, who considered it their duty to not remain silent, did it. My husband and I had to do it too".*

They continued to cover the repressions.

In May 2016, the first searches in Bakhchysarai were held. Seyran Saliyev informed people in the mosque on the microphone who was being searched. In July he was fined 20 thousand rubles for allegedly organizing an unsanctioned rally.

Mumine recalled: *"On January 26, 2017, we were sleeping. It was around four o'clock in the morning. All of a sudden there was a knock on the door and shouting that they were going to break it. So, we opened the door. Around 10-15 men with a dog walked in. They were all wearing balaclavas and had no chevrons. The reason was not announced. It was the so-called Centre for Combating Extremism. They turned whole our apartment upside down".*

Then there was the first punishment — the administrative one. Seyran Saliyev faced 12 days in a detention center.

"When he got out, I told him that it was a distress signal. You should either leave Crimea or stay quiet. Are you ready to resist? He said that he was neither going to stay silent nor to leave. He could not escape and pretend that nothing was happening. And it was important for me to understand, whether he is ready. I was thinking to myself: if he is ready, then I am ready too. If he turned out to be not ready, I would not be able to take everything on myself without his support. And then he was sent to prison".

During the five years without her husband, Mumine was not just working on defending him. She realized that she lacked professional knowledge of journalism, so she entered and finished an extramural course at the faculty of international journalism at the Yaroslav Mudryi Odessa Law Academy. The education helped her to not only master the standards of the profession, but also taught her to realize her ideas.

And life itself threw her the ideas.

During the search, FSB officers injured Mumine's seven-year-old daughter Samiya. Her head was hit and she got terribly scared. Later doctors diagnosed her with juvenile idiopathic arthritis. This has affected her mental health and her somatics. Her legs began to swell. She could not walk normally. Now her illness requires treatment with anti-cancer drugs.

Two of the three daughters of Ruslan Zeytullayev also developed behavioral changes due to stress. They did not speak and refused to eat.

In December 2014, Rustem Vaitov was married, and on January 23, 2015, he was arrested. The couple didn't have enough time to enjoy married life. The door to their home was locked with a simple hook. Uninvited guests were able to unlock it easily. As the security forces walked in, the couple was sleeping in their bed. His wife Aliye woke up with a gun held next to her temple by a security officer.

Then he pointed a gun at her stomach. After Rustem's arrest it turned out that his wife was pregnant. When the fetus was six months old, during a medical examination doctors discovered various pathologies and suggested Aliye have an abortion. Her religious beliefs forbid doing so. The girl Safiko was born sick and after her birth she underwent two dozen surgeries.

"I talked to Khadija Ismayilova. In her family at first her father and then grandfather and uncle were arrested" Mumine Saliyeva told Ukrinform agency on March 18, 2021. "This family was de-facto deprived of men. Then Khadija suddenly said to me: "Do you want to see my diary?" This is the diary, in which girls write down their secrets and don't tell anyone about them. So, every page of Khadija's diary was dedicated to her father. There were drawings – she drew her father, there were stories about successes, lines about how much she missed her father. Also, the following was written there: "Today I got really upset, but if you were here, you would definitely support me". I wanted to cry, but I held my tears back. I see that many children associate all their thoughts, dreams and successes to their fathers. Children see us, their caregivers, as their family members and share their feelings with us."

"Another 12 children were born after the arrest of their fathers" says Mumine. *"In general, 204 kids are growing up without a father. 58 of them have complicated diagnoses, triggered by the arrests of their parents. I decided that this problem should somehow be combined on one platform, in order to provide these children with comprehensive assistance. We hold monthly meetings [Crimean Childhood]. We call them intellectual courses."*

"We do not intend to replace the system of education and learning. At the intellectual courses we divide children into age groups, conduct trainings, master classes, quests, give lessons on the history of Crimean Tatars and Crimea, logic and the Crimean Tatar language. Master classes are held in online and offline forms. The main goal is for them to not feel abandoned and to ensure this repressive machine won't break, won't make them embittered, so that they remain people with kind hearts".

Here is what Khalide, the wife of the political prisoner and journalist Remzi Bekirov, said: *"The meetings of the „Crimean Childhood" are special. Children miss each other very much. Sea of emotions and impressions stay in kids' memories for a long time. New useful knowledge, quizzes, workshops and gifts add colors to their childhood".*

In addition, as part of the Crimean Childhood meetings, online classes are held in English language, mathematics, and drawing lessons.

Saifullah, the son of the political prisoner Eldar Kantimirov, has been working with the Crimean Childhood teacher for six months. Here is his mother's comment about this: „*The classes are held in an entertaining form and my son likes them a lot. The teacher sparks kids' interest and these classes help a lot in improving their language".*

Mumine talks about this in social networks and writes articles. There are a lot of people, who, according to her words, drop off food for the children, sometimes buy them lunches or transfer money for them, and psychologists provide their services free of charge.

She has created several projects dedicated to these kids. "Born After Arrest" is a photo exhibition with stories about children, the fathers of whom were arrested even before the births of their daughters and sons. The exhibition took place in Kyiv with the assistance of the Ukrainian Helsinki Human Rights Union.

There is also a page on Facebook called Crimean Childhood, which is dedicated to the children of political prisoners. Under the same name, another photo exhibition was held in the capital of Ukraine.

This activity has annoyed the occupying government.

On May 30, 2019, near her house on Mira Street in Bakhchysarai, the officers of the so-called Centre for Combating Extremism forced Mumine to get into a car and took her to their office in Simferopol. She spent a whole day there without a lawyer. Mumine said that she was made to understand that she should stay at home and remain silent and that no one would then touch her. The next day the so-called Kyivskyi District Court of Simferopol fined Mumine 1000 rubles for a post on Facebook that was dated 2013 (that is the time when Crimea was still part of Ukraine and under the control of Kyiv).

Thanks to education and practice, Mumine Saliyeva turned from an amateur journalist into a professional one. She publishes articles in media outlets, joined the National Union of Journalists of Ukraine and has a press card from the European Federation of Journalists.

For her volunteer activity, Mumine has received an award from the public organization "Euromaidan SOS" and the Order of Princess Olga from the president of Ukraine. However, despite all her activity, she has not forgotten her imprisoned husband. As soon as the opportunity arose, she, with all family members, visited him for several days, where under prison conditions they could pray with their whole family after five years apart. Mumine very touchingly described this reunion on her Facebook page.

"It is time for an afternoon prayer. Seyran tells his son: "perform salah", and his eyes are filling with tears again, as he says: "I was waiting for so long for my son to grow up and perform salah. And now it is happening…" The last time we had a joint family prayer on the day of his arrest – on October 11, 2017. And now, five years later, we did it as a whole family again. The taste of faith, the gratitude to God for His mercy were overflowing. Oh, how I missed this: humbly standing in prayer behind by husband, feeling the protection, safety and tranquility.

Three days were not enough to talk. There was so much I wanted to tell and to hear. I saw a noble, strong-willed person. Seyran studied many chapters of the Holy Quran, told many sayings of the Prophet Muhammad (pbuh), stories from the lives of scientists. He told how difficult the stages of convoying from the Ufa pre-detention center to the Tula colony were. He asked a lot about the situation of the people, news, Bakhchysarai. I had an impression that he didn't forget anyone or anything to ask about. My dearest husband hasn't changed for worse even a bit even under such inhuman conditions. Thanks to his patience he acquired the best, as the senior companion Umar ibn Al-Khattab (r.a.) said. „You know, it feels like these five years never happened, I tell him. – The pain is gone. The relief appears to be so great, that the complications and the burden of challenges are forgotten.

I don't remember, where was the last time I was flying around the kitchen and cooking different meals with such a joy. Turns out that cooking for family is a whole different, special feeling, which I completely forgot how to feel over these years. The kids were happy. They did not leave their father for a single step".

"FSS are ruling in Crimea, and this is the axiom"

On April 6, 2021, Vladyslav Yesypenko, the freelance correspondent of Crimea.Realities, a project of Radio Free Europe/Radio Liberty (RFE/RL), wrote a statement addressed to his lawyers Emil Kurbedinov, Taras Omelchenko and Alexey Ladin. In it, he described the torture that he underwent at the hands of officers of the Russian Federal Security Service.

Here is the full text of his statement:

"My name is Vladyslav Yesypenko. On my way back from Simferopol to Alushta I was detained by the officers of Federal Security Service of Russia. As the result of the search, the officers of FSS have planted a grenade into my car, Škoda Rapid. After the search I refused to sign any documents but was told that they are now going to take me to some other place, where I will sign anything. After that they put a bag over my head, put me in the car and in about an hour brought me to some basement with no windows. In this basement, the FSS officers (they all wore balaclavas) forcefully stripped me naked (I once read, that in Nazi concentration camps, in order for victims to lose the ability to resist, they were also being stripped naked). After that I was laid on the floor and had two loops attached to my ears, wires from which led to an object, which looked similar to TAP-57 army field phone. After that they ran electric current through these wires.

The pain was very bad, it felt like eyes were exploding fire and the brain was boiling. Because of such pain I was ready to confess in anything and sign any papers. They tortured me whole night, asked if I was connected to any special services. During the break they took me to the toilet and gave me water to drink, then electricity was replaced with beating by FSS officers. However, they did not hit my head, they aimed at my stomach, legs and genitals. In the morning I testified on camera and signed some documents.

On the next day, without lawyers, I was taken to the area of the city of Armiansk for the investigative actions, where I was pointed to the place, where I allegedly picked up the grenade. After that the FSS officers explained to me that I should not hire private lawyers and sign testimony at the investigator, or else I will be tortured again, but the next time electric wires will be connected to my genitals, not my ears. Until today, due to pressure I was unable to change the lawyer and was forced to sign the testimony against myself".

Later in court, Yesypenko would tell much more terrible details of how he was treated by the officers of the Russian Federal Security Service.

On February 16, 2022, Yesypenko was sentenced to six years' imprisonment in an ordinary regime colony and was fined 110 thousand rubles for the illegal storage and transportation of an explosive device. The Russian prosecution had requested 11 years behind bars for the journalist.

No audience was allowed to attend the trial in the Kremlin-controlled court.

During his final speech on the day before the sentence Yesypenko said that he considers this case to be a political one.

"Why? Because I am a journalist of the Ukrainian outlet and, most likely, Federal Security Service officers wanted to demonstrate, how much unacceptable the freedom of speech is. I think that threats and tortures are not acceptable in XXI century. In 1937 my grandfather was tortured and shot. I got an impression that those Chekists, who were there back then, they have grandchildren and great-grandchildren, who are doing the same things as were done in 1937.

If my verdict will not be acquittal, then I believe that it is a verdict to the system, because FSS are ruling in Crimea", as quoted to Crimea.Realities (RFE/RL).

He also added that evidently the FSS are ruling in Crimea, stressing that this will not change.

When Yesypenko mentioned the execution of his grandfather, he meant the repression during Stalin's time, when the NKVD (People's Commissariat for Internal Affairs) investigators tortured arrested innocent people to get testimonials. Based on such testimonials, Soviet courts pronounced verdicts. These were either deportation to the GULAG camps, or execution by firing squad. (The grandfather of the author of these lines was also executed in 1937, as was their grandfather's brother.)

Kateryna Yesypenko, the wife of the political prisoner, says that Vladyslav's grandfather was 42 years old when he was executed. He was arrested for spying. A cow and a house were taken from his family. Five children were left orphans. His wife had to dig a Zemlyanka (earth-house) in the ground in which to live. Now Vladyslav faced the same treatment.

On August 18, 2022, the Russian-controlled "Supreme Court of Crimea" mitigated the sentence for Yesypenko to five years of imprisonment in an ordinary regime colony, with a 110 thousand rubles fine.

Vladyslav Yesypenko was born and lived until 2013 in the industrial city of Kryvyi Rih in the Dnipropetrovsk region, where heavy industry is located. The city is situated 345 kilometers southeast of Kyiv. Vladyslav owned a business in real estate. In Kryvyi Rih, the ecology is not very good and the level of air pollution can reach a point at which it is hard to breathe. He dreamt of moving to Crimea, which has a mild climate, sea and wonderful nature. After getting married in 2012, he told his wife Kateryna about this dream and the family moved to Sevastopol. It is the city in which, since the collapse of the Soviet Union, the Russian Black Sea Fleet is based. Ukraine and Russia concluded an agreement about the presence of the Black Sea Fleet on Ukrainian territory. (Currently, there is a consensus in Ukraine that it was one of the biggest mistakes of the Ukrainian independence period.)

"We moved there approximately at the end of 2012 or the beginning of 2013" says Kateryna Yesypenko.

"We bought an apartment in Sevastopol on Henerala Vakulenchuka Street. Turned it into our family nest. A magnificent panorama of Striletska bay was seen from our window.

In Sevastopol there were many military units – both Ukrainian and Russian.

Even in the yard of our apartment building there was a military unit. When the occupation began, I saw with my own eyes how Ukrainian military units were blocked. „Little green men" without any identification marks stood in our yard, there were also some men in the blue uniform – apparently, they were from the Russian police. Back then I did not know for sure.

At that time Vladyslav was filming with his phone a lot. From one side there were our boys, who were blocked. From the other side, the crowd of the Nakhimov square, who were shouting "Russia! Russia!".

He filmed without any specific goal; he made it for himself. He also gave interviews to the foreign mass media. He was against such brutal actions of Russians. My husband told me that we should leave this place, because he didn't want to live in stinking Sovok (The word „sovok" in Ukraine is used as a derogatory name for the Soviet Union – Y. L.) and under Putin's ruling.

But I was pregnant back then and was simply scared to get in trouble and cause harm to the baby. Because on the way to the mainland Ukraine there were checkpoints, where the so-called "Crimea's self-defense forces" acted arbitrarily. That is why we decided to postpone our departure.

On July 28 our daughter Stefania was born. At the maternity hospital they asked me why my daughter has such a Ukrainian name. The pro-Russian hysteria there was getting frenzy, as even the name, common not only in Ukraine, but in the whole world, aroused suspicions.

We left Crimea at the end of 2014 or the beginning of 2015. We moved our belongings in two stages. Back then there was still chaos, we took our daughter out without any documents, having only the certificate from the maternity hospital. Our cats were transported without documents as well.

We sold our apartment. When selling real estate there, you need to pay around 3 percent of tax. For the foreigners, and we were already foreigners in our country, the tax was around 14 percent. The difference was significant. We lost a lot. But we came back to Kryvyi Rih".

According to Kateryna's words, her husband could not accept the fact that Russians occupied that part of Ukrainian territory. He decided to do something about this situation. Yesypenko went to Kyiv and offered to show the videos that he filmed in Crimea. Kateryna says that at that time interest in this topic had worn off a bit, therefore mass media were not much interested. However, he discovered the Radio Liberty project called Crimea.Realities (RFE/RL).

"He contacted our presenter Olexander Yankovsky" says Volodymyr Prytula, the chief editor of Crimea.Realities (RFE/RL). *"He connected him with our TV crew. Vladyslav told them that he travels to Crimea on his business and can film for us. People who go there are important for us. He was explained what needs to be filmed and how – polling, landscapes, environmental things, for example he was filming Bakalska split for us. We never asked him to take videos of military objects. Of course, we explained all risks. I was not the one to contact him, our TV producers did".*

According to Kateryna Yesypenko, during his trips her husband regularly called her and shared his impressions. On March 9, 2021, he told her that he was at a rally in honor of the birthday of the great Ukrainian poet Taras Shevchenko. He said that the participants of the rally were surrounded by police officers, who were filming the event. He was filming too. Vladyslav thought that he was captured on video too.

And on the next day, on March 10, Vladyslav did not get in touch with his wife.

"I began to worry", Kateryna Yesypenko recalls. *"I tried to call the police and other government authorities. But calls to those numbers from Ukraine were blocked. I called the Russian embassy in Kyiv, informed them that my husband went missing. I asked if they could inform the police. They refused. I was advised to send an email to the police, FSS and other authorities. I wrote them. They responded to me exactly in 30 days, as it should be done by their law. They told me what I already knew by that time.*

I informed the editorial office of Crimea.Realities (RFE/RL) about the disappearance of my husband. They connected the lawyer, Emil Kurbedinov. He began looking for Vladyslav but could not find him".

According to the chief editor of Crimea.Realities (RFE/RL), Volodymyr Prytula, he didn't even know Yesypenko's first name, he only knew his nickname and never communicated with him personally. *"It is being done for the sake of safety. The smaller number of people know the freelancer – the lower are the risks. But he knows the names of the lawyers, who can provide him with legal protection in case of a critical situation.*

On the next day I got a call from Crimea. The Lawyer Violetta Sineglazova called me. She said that Vladyslav had been arrested, but he was doing fine. She informed me cheerfully that they even smoked with him on a backyard of Federal Security Service office. The fact itself, that it was happening not even in police, but in FSS, was not much soothing.

I asked her why he was arrested. She replied that she cannot disclose that.

"If you want to know, come here", she invited me. "I will arrange a meeting for you". She even invited me to come with my child. I believe that if I came, I would have been detained, so they could influence my husband through me.

I asked her, how many years he is facing. She replied: from 8 to 10 years, but he will get 6. She said that tomorrow the court will select the preventive measure. I was told about the money. As I understood, she was a double agent. However, I asked her, if she would work on this case with bigger interest, if we signed legal services agreement, and how much it would cost. She said that she is ready to represent his interests in court on a paid basis – it would cost 100 thousand rubles.

At the same time, she informed me that Vladyslav was arrested on March 11, and not March 10. As I found out later, on the night between March 10th and 11th he was being tortured. Apparently by shifting the date, she wanted to hide the fact of torture.

I asked her if she saw the traces of beating on Vladyslav. She assured me, referring to her lawyer's honor, that there was nothing like that. Later it turned out that she lied.

She is a state lawyer, which means that she was appointed by the occupying state. I have no doubts she is working for FSS and not defending clients. We never talked again".

Later in court Vladyslav Yesypenko talked about the role of the lawyer Sineglazova.

"When I was going on a business trip, I was told that I can name the lawyer if any problems occur, that I can request to see specifically him" (Apparently the recommendations were given by the editorial office of the Crimea.Realities (RFE/RL) – Y. L.). *"I explained to the investigator*

Vlasov, that I want the other lawyer, not the one they appointed, but Emil Kurbedinov or Taras Omelchenko. I haven't met them, but I knew that they could help me. But the investigator Vlasov explained to me, that it was not possible, that I have only one lawyer appointed – Violetta Sineglazova and there can be no other options.

At some point the lawyer Sineglazova and I went outside for a smoke break. I explained to her that I was tortured, that I had burns behind my ears left with electrical wires, to which she did not react in any way. She did not submit protests or claims. The only thing she did was explaining to me that she had similar cases and if I incriminated myself and testified, I would face a maximum of three years in prison and parole afterwards. And, of course, the investigator supported Sineglazova's position.

At that moment I realized that as long as I had an appointed lawyer, there are no options to somehow defend myself, thus I signed the documents. In addition, during the investigative actions and later, when we were on our way back from Armiansk, I was being threatened. In other words, they pressured me morally and psychologically and explained that if I "sham stupidity" as they say in slang, I will be dead before the trial. I understood that and, until I had the opportunity to meet the lawyers, I was giving 'testimony'".

Later, a lawyer Alexey Ladin appealed to the Crimean Chamber of Lawyers with a complaint regarding the actions of Violetta Sineglazova. The complaint was reviewed, but they did not pass judgement on her. Vladyslav Yesypenko managed to meet with the lawyers provided by the human rights defenders, and he refused any further services of Sineglazova.

RFE/RL's Crimea.Realities learned about Sineglazova's past. At some point she used to work as a newscaster on the Crimean TV channel Chernomorka, which moved to Kyiv after the occupation of the Peninsula. However, Sineglazova had by then left television and she became an assistant of a lawyer. In 2012 she got a law degree. After the occupation she received a Russian lawyer's certificate.

Olha Skrypnyk, the head of the Crimean Human Rights Group, faced Sineglazova's activity previously.

"Violetta Sineglazova always represents interests of the investigation, and not the defendant", she says. *„She gets appointed to similar cases so that she could persuade people to sign testimonies even regarding something they never did."*

I sent a message through WhatsApp and Viber to the number listed on Sineglazova's Facebook profile, asking questions regarding her position. She never responded.

On March 12, 2021, the trial was held, where they chose a preventive measure for Vladyslav Yesypenko.

According to the testimony of the lawyer Emil Kurbedinov, he could not be present at the trial, since he was not informed and there was no information about it on the websites. The judge of the Kyivskyi District Court of Simferopol, Viktor Krapko, chose detention as a preventive measure for Yesypenko.

After learning about the verdict of the "court" on March 15, Kurbedinov headed to the detention facility, but was shown a waiver of his service signed by Yesypenko. Kurbedinov asked the lawyer Alexey Ladin to take over the case.

Ladin stated that on March 12, 2021, ten-ish minutes after his arrival at the detention facility, the FSS investigator Vlasov appeared. Ladin was hindered during the registration of documents (apparently, they were needed for access to the detention facility — Y. L.). A duty officer who was supposed to take him to the investigator delayed Ladin's access to his office. Afterwards, the head of the detention facility's special unit explained to Ladin that Yesypenko had signed a document in which he refused to have Ladin as his lawyer. According to Ladin, this is what the head of the detention facility told her. However, Ladin could not speak to him, as he was "too busy". *"It is obvious that the officials are committing flagrant violations"*, Ladin summarized.

Kateryna recalled *"My husband seemed to have been found, however nobody saw him. There was no certainty that he was alive. I talked to Crimean activists. They suggested me to take an inmate package to the detention facility. If they accept it, then it means he is there. My Crimean assistant bought the essentials: a toothbrush, toothpaste, soap, sugar, tea, household chemicals. They accepted the package. I sighed with relief, if the word "relief" can be used in this situation. After all, it was unbelievable that in XXI century you should use such wild methods to find out where the human is imprisoned".*

On March 18, on TV channel Crimea-24 a report appeared in which Vladyslav Yesypenko was answering questions from a journalist. In the introduction to the report, it said that *"the American media holding scrutinizes the Ukrainian president. The journalist of the RFE/RL's "Crimea.Realities", a part of "Radio Liberty", which is financed and fully controlled by the States, was appointed task to make a journalistic investigation about the Crimean apartment of Volodymyr Zelensky".*

This formulation of the question indicates the difference in the worldviews informing Ukrainian and Russian journalism and, apparently, their audience. The Russian TV channel presents this as a terrible conspiracy of insidious Americans against the Ukrainian president. Meanwhile, it is quite normal for Ukraine to investigate the activity of Ukrainian heads of state. Not only are employees of Radio Liberty, which is financed by the United States, but other media outlets are also doing so at their own initiative.

The fact that this interview was undertaken by the general producer of the TV channel Crimea-24 Oleg Kryuchkov — the former correspondent of the Ukrainian TV channel Novyi Kanal on the Crimean Peninsula — and not by another journalist, indicates the importance of this material for Russian propaganda. Yesypenko stated that he used to cooperate with the Security Service of Ukraine, and with one of its executives, Viktor Kravchuk. This cooperation involved providing the Security Service of Ukraine with the material that he had filmed for Radio Liberty. The interviewer had no questions arising from this; the security service apparently needed him to send materials, which were already publicly available.

"It was obvious for everyone who knew Vladyslav, that there was something wrong with him" says Kateryna Yesypenko, *"that it wasn't of his own free will that he was making such confessions. I saw bruises on his face and neck.*

It was only the third lawyer who managed to see Vladyslav at the detention facility. He told him that he was being looked after. Because my husband was in the informational isolation, the FSS wanted to create the impression that no one needed him. Vlad managed to write a "kite" (this is what they call a note in prison slang—Y. L.) *for me".*

Vladyslav wrote to his wife: *"At first, I denied everything. And when they took me to the court to choose a preventive measure for me, I used the article 51 of Constitution of the Russian Federation"* (this article allows people to refuse giving testimony against themselves—Y. L.). *"But FSS found the "arguments" for me to start testifying against myself to the investigator and in front of TV cameras.*

You should not visit me, as you can become a hostage to this situation, and I do not want that for you, even though I miss you and Stesha a lot.

I also wanted to say that they force me to reject the lawyers, they insist that my interests in court should be presented by the lawyer Sineglazova V., and this woman is their decoy. Therefore, I have no idea yet, how to change this situation.

But I'm not giving up and keep my head up. With my cellmate we train twice a day, and during the one-hour walk in the afternoon we run 2km. He calls me sensei. Whenever we have free time, we read books and study. I want to believe that in the nearest future an exchange between Ukraine and Russia will be held and I will be able to come back home. But if this doesn't happen, I am convinced that I can handle everything and will not give up…

… Thank you for your support, my dear. I know that you will not give up. Probably, only being here, I realized how much I love you and Stesha".

Volodymyr Prytula commented: *"It took a long time for us to decide whether it would harm Yesypenko if we disclosed that he was from Crimea.Realities, because even the suspicion about his cooperation with us could make his situation worse. And at first, we had no idea, what he was arrested for. Earlier, several of our special correspondents were released after getting arrested, because they didn't know that those people were related to RFE/RL's Crimea.Realities. They were simply fined for the "illegal activity" and expelled from Crimea. Ultimately, we decided that we should emphasize that he worked as a journalist and filmed for us. Publicity could help protect him".*

The first trial session of the court, where the merits of the case were reviewed, was held on July 15, 2021. For journalists, access to the courtroom was limited; only one person was allowed, Lutfiye Zudiyeva, the correspondent of the website Hraty (Bars), described the process in detail, and did a great job.

The case was reviewed by the „Simferopol district Court". The judge Dlyaver Berberov presided over the trial. The website of the public movement „Chesno" has him listed in the Register of State Traitors. A criminal proceeding was opened against Berberov in Ukraine on the suspicion of treason for violating of the oath of the judge.

The description of his case says: „Despite the requirements of the Ukrainian legislation, in violation of the Oath [of] the judge, after the annexation of the Crimean Peninsula by the Russian Federation, starting from March 2014, this judge began to deliver "justice" in so-called courts of the Republic of Crimea and make the illegal court decisions.

"In November–December 2014, in accordance with the decrees of the President of the aggressor country "On the appointment the federal judges", he transferred to the service in the illegally created courts. The cynicism of these "servants of Themis" lies in the fact that almost during the whole year of 2014, while making court decisions "in the name of Russian Federation", they certified the legitimacy of the same decisions with the Ukrainian seal". (At first, after the occupation there were simply no seals of the Russian federation in the courts, thus the „judges" used the Ukrainian ones—Y. L.).

"At the first session of the court the "prosecutor" Elena Podolnaya announced an indictment. She was a former employee of the prosecutor's office of the Crimean Autonomous Republic of Ukraine. She betrayed the oath and transferred to the service of the occupiers. On May 14, 2015, the Prosecutor General of Ukraine declared their suspicion of her under the article "State treason"."

The indictment read:

"The investigation believes that Vladyslav Yesypenko, while planning his trip to Crimea to work as a freelance journalist for „Crimea.Realities", accepted the offer of an identified person to get the RGD-5 hand grenade from the cache not far from Pravda village of Pervomaiske district – "to ensure the personal safety"."

In the testimony, which according to Yesypenko the FSS officers beat out of him, it was said that the cache was prepared by the Foreign Intelligence Service of Ukraine, with whom Yesypenko allegedly cooperated. However, it was not included in the indictment.

As evidence, the prosecution attached Yesypenko's interview with the producer and journalist of the TV channel Crimea-24, Oleg Kryuchkov, as well as all of Yesypenko's initial testimony, to the case file. He insisted that both interview and testimony were given under torture.

At the second session, on September 6, 2021, Yesypenko was surprised with the FSS version, according to which, after his arrest he was released with an obligation to come back the next day. *"If I am the agent of the Security Service of Ukraine, this involves espionage, nobody would release me per se"*, he said. He recalled that they had surveillance cameras in the Federal Security Service office, which should have filmed him being taken out.

Kateryna Yesypenko said: *"When I found out about this, I immediately recalled the words of the pseudo-lawyer Sineglazova, who was assuring me over the phone, that he got arrested a day later than it actually happened. Now I was sure that in such way she was trying to hide the fact of tortures".*

According to the investigation materials, the grenade, which was allegedly found during Yesypenko's arrest, was stored in the glove compartment of his car. At the same time, the length of the grenade is 14 centimeters, while the width of the glove compartment is 12 centimeters. In other words, the grenade is 2 cm longer and would simply not fit in the glove compartment. Furthermore, Yesypenko's fingerprints were not found on the grenade.

Numerous procedural violations were listed in court, the main one being the denial of access to lawyers for Yesypenko. The procedural violation should have led to an acquittal, as envisaged by the law. However, it did not happen.

Prosecutor Elena Podolnaya said during the trial: *"I ask the court to find Vladyslav Yesypenko fully guilty, under part one of article 223 of the Criminal Code of the Russian Federation* (Illegal Manufacture of Weapons — Y. L.) *and sentence him to 9 years of imprisonment with 200 thousand rubles fine. Also I find him guilty under part one of article 222 of the Criminal Code of the Russian Federation* (Illegal Acquisition, Transfer, Sale, Storage, Transportation, or Bearing of Firearms, Its Basic Parts, Ammunition, Explosives, and Explosive Devices — Y. L.) *and sentence him to 7 years of imprisonment and 50 thousand rubles fine. In total through the cumulation sentence him to 11 years in prison with 200 thousand rubles fine"*.

Yesypenko wrote to his wife from the pre-trial detention center: *"Hello, Katrusia! Today is February 16. It is 1 a.m.. The trial session ended. It would be an understatement to say that I was surprised about the fact that the prosecutor requested the 11 years of sentence. I understood that FSS officers would take revenge for my position, but I definitely did not expect such a number. I am worried about you, about your condition. It was my decision to prove my case in court. You supported it. Thank you. I want to say it once again. Now it's up to my country. We did everything we could. I hope that I, as well as the other political prisoners, will not be forgotten…"*.

The court sentenced him to a six-year term, which had been predicted by the "lawyer" Violetta Sineglazova during her phone call with Kateryna Yesypenko, and which six months later was reduced to one year.

The president of Radio Liberty, Jamie Fly, commented on Yesypenko's verdict: *"This trial on Vladyslav is a parody. Since journalists do nothing else but inform about facts, he should never have been arrested on the first place, and even more so — subjected to physical and psychological tortures, which he experienced over the last 11 months. Vladyslav should be returned home to his wife and daughter immediately."*

On September 1, 2022, Vladyslav Yesypenko was sent to serve his prison sentence in penal colony No. 2 in the Crimean city of Kerch.

A number of public human rights organizations followed this case. On July 6, 2021, they held a rally in Kyiv, in support of Vladyslav Yesypenko. Later they set up a campaign on social networks with hashtags #JournalismIsNotaCrime, #FreeYesypenko and #PrisonersVoice. ZMINA, Crimean Human Rights Group, Ukrainian Helsinki Human Rights Union and other organizations supported Kateryna and her daughter.

On May 25, 2022, in New York, the world-known actor Michael Douglas presented Kateryna Yesypenko the American PEN/Barbey—Freedom to Write Award. The „Freedom to Write" award was established in 2016 specifically for authors who are imprisoned for their work.

"My husband has been in prison for 15 months only because he is a journalist. Vladyslav knew, that reporting from Crimea, which is occupied by Russia, was dangerous, but he believed that people deserve to know what was happening there, to know the truth. He also believes that it is important to tell the stories, which usually don't make it into headlines or the front pages," said Kateryna during the ceremony, to which she came with her daughter Stefania, or as her father affectionately calls her, Stesha.

***

Before the beginning of the Russian Federation's full-scale invasion of Ukraine, 12 journalists were imprisoned in Crimea. These are Crimean Tatar civic journalists: Osman Arifmemetov, Marlen (Suleyman) Asanov, Asan Akhtemov, Remzi Bekirov, Tymur Ibrahimov, Server Mustafayev, Seyran Saliyev, Amet Suleymanov, Ruslan Suleymanov and Rustem Sheykhaliyev, as well as journalists Oleksiy Bessarabov and Vladyslav Yesypenko. After February 24, 2022, Russia imprisoned two more civic journalists, Vilen Temeryanov and Iryna Danylovych. Due to politically motivated persecution, the First Deputy Chairman of the Mejlis of the Crimean Tatar People and former journalist Nariman Dzhelial is also in prison.

The Last Word

What is happening in „Russian" Crimea?

Foreign journalists as the instruments of Russian propaganda

During communist dictator Joseph Stalin's rule in the USSR, he invited western intellectuals and journalists to the Soviet Union, to take part in trips around the country, where he showed them what were called "Potemkin villages".

This label has historical roots. It relates to Count Grigory Potemkin, a favorite of the Russian empress Catherine the Great. On the path that laid out the queen's route through Ukraine he built fake villages. The villages were decorated with triumphal arches and huts were painted and decorated with an excessive number of flowers. The goal was to create the impression for the queen that the people there lived rich and prosperous lives.

Stalin's guests returned back home with glowing tributes to the USSR. This was in 1933 when Russian policies created an artificial famine (later known in Ukraine as Holodomor), which resulted in the deaths of at least six million people. Stalin used to call such Western "helpers" "convenient idiots".

Modern Russia also resorts to the same methods.

In July 2016 I received information that the Russian propagandist tv channel Russia Today (RT) had invited the representatives of the mass media from different countries to visit Crimea. It financed that trip, which started on July 16.

The organization of such trips was a result of the Russian government taking strict measures of limiting access to Crimea for foreign journalists, but Moscow was interested in international public opinion being favorable toward Crimea being part of Russia. Therefore they organized this press tour.

Russia Today listed Elizaveta Isakova as the manager of this group. According to Google search results, the person with such a

name delivered the news for another Russian propagandist resource RIA Novosti (RIA News) from Geneva.

In the list, which was received from trustworthy sources, there
were 15 mass-media outlets. It featured the French Radio Zones, the
American Independent Newspaper Group, the Mexican Televista
Monterrey, Radio Métropole based in Haiti, the Brazilian *Globo News*
and *Correio do Brasil*, the Indian magazine *Governance Now* and *Dec-
can Herald*, the Portuguese *EspressoLisbonne*, Switzerland's *Le Temps*,
and a journal *Russian Switzerland* based either in Russia or in Switzerland. Additionally, there were French radio and Deutsche Welle.

It looked like an adventure because the journalists had to arrive on the Peninsula from the Russian side, without getting permission from the Ukrainian government — thus violating Ukrainian
laws. The permission to visit Crimea was stipulated by the Law of
Ukraine „On Ensuring the Rights and Freedoms of Citizens and the
Legal Regime on the Temporarily Occupied Territory of Ukraine".

A conversation with one of the group members confirmed
they had no idea about this law. I found the email addresses of all
media outlets on the list and sent them an email with a warning. I
have no idea if all of the invited outlets did participate, however the
trip did take place.

The email stated: *"Dear Colleagues! It has come to my attention from
trustworthy sources that on July 16, a group of journalists from different
countries are going to the occupied Crimea in a trip organized by Russia
Today. Rebranded as RT to conceal its origins from the unsuspecting, it is
not a news or media outlet. It is the international propaganda arm of the
Russian government whose sole purpose is serving the Kremlin.*

*I am writing to you because journalists representing your organiza-
tion has been listed as participants in the RT-led group. While I respect
your choice, I strongly disagree with it and wish to inform you of its dangers.*

*First: The RT-led group will enter Crimea from Russia. This is a
violation of Ukrainian law, which requires Kyiv's permission to visit the
occupied peninsula. It also carries the risk of being blacklisted from entering Ukraine in the future.*

Second: By entering Crimea under the aegis of RT, your journalists will be under the control of the Kremlin's chief propaganda purveyor and will not be able to collect objective information. It is possible to report objectively even under those conditions – but only if it is made clear that reporters were shown only what RT, and, therefore, the Russian government – wanted them to see. Otherwise, your publication becomes a pawn in the Kremlin propaganda wars.

Third: If your journalists plan to meet with sources independently while they are in Crimea, I must warn you that they will be putting those sources at risk from the Russian security services. Repression against any sort of dissidence or independent voices in Crimea is severe since its annexation by Moscow.

I can provide you with documentation, including the European Federation of Journalists' condemnation of the increasing repression against journalists there. Objective reporting about occupied Crimea is crucial. But I firmly believe that a reporting trip organized by RT, Russia's chief propaganda arm, is unlikely to produce it".

Afterwards I discovered two publications about Crimea which were written in English by journalists who were on one of these trips As it turned out, there were more than one press tour.

On August 1, 2016, Indian journalist Shreerupa Mitra-Jha posted an article on the website *Governance Now* with the subtitle "Why crisis diplomacy is urgently needed between Russia and the West to temper down the heat building up in the Black Sea peninsula". The subtitle implies that the problem of Crimea is related to Russia and the West, and not Ukraine, which had lost this part of its territory and therefore was not a subject.

However, the author balanced her report. She presented the point of view of a Crimean official, who said that the referendum took place and the majority of Crimean residents voted for joining Russia. But she also stated that the USA, EU, and Ukraine do not recognize Crimea as part of the Russian Federation. However, in her text, she presented it as simply a difference in views on the problem, which often happens in the world of politics. No emphasis was made that in this case it is generally recognized by the world community that Crimea had been seized by force with a brutal violation of international legislation and that the referendum was an imitation of free will, since it was held at gunpoint and violated the law.

The author presented the point of view of an anonymous 20-year-old Crimean Tatar who did not agree with Crimea being a part of Russia. However, there was no mention of the repression against dissenters, and nothing about the persecution of Crimean Tatars, with no descriptions of the systematic violations of human rights.

On July 29, the American journalist Corey Flintoff published a report titled "The View from A Russian Frigate in Crimea", on the website NPR (National Public Radio). The author described the construction of a new frigate as a response to "threats" from NATO. He stated that both sides had tense relations and were arming themselves.

The frigate's captain — Anatoly Velichko — told Flintoff that his 'warfare mission' is to "fight other ships at sea and to destroy any coastal installations", but the journalist reported that he was not allowed to see any of the ship's machinery or electronics.

In some reports, other journalists do not mention that they were in Crimea at the expense of the Russian side. Russia attempted to dupe these journalists and use their presence as part of its propaganda.

On August 15, 2016, on the Facebook page of the Ministry of Foreign Affairs of Ukraine, an apology was posted from the then head of the Moscow bureau of the German Deutsche Welle news outlet Juri Rescheto. Earlier he had been on a trip, organized by Russia, after which Russia Today quoted him on July 8, 2016, as saying: *"We have seen some positive developments here … people tell me about many things in their daily life getting better,"* Juri Rescheto, the head of the German Deutsche Welle Moscow office, told RT, stressing that he saw *"many positive developments … particularly for the local residents"* during his visit. He also emphasized that *"Crimea now became a Russian territory regardless of whether we [the West] want it or not,"* adding that *"it is now a fact, a reality"*.

In addition, he posted few tweets with the hashtag #crimeaisrussia, which was noted by Ukrainian journalist Dmytro Homonay:

"In his posts, Rescheto was using hashtags #Russia and #Crimea, but never – #Ukraine. He deleted all those posts after the beginning of the scandal, but concerned people managed to take screenshots in time," — noted Homonay on August 17, 2016, on the website of the Ukrainian TV channel Espreso.

In one of his tweets Rescheto wrote: *"I am leaving Moscow for an exciting trip across six regions of Russia for the Russian edition of DW – we are starting from Crimea".*

In other words, according to this logic, Crimea is a region of the Russian Federation. However, the vast majority of countries in the world do not recognize the annexation of the Peninsula by Russia, including Germany.

Homonay's article stated that the first person who noted the scandalous posts of Russia Today and Rescheto was the head of the Ukrainian office of the Heinrich Böll Foundation in Kyiv, Serhii Sumlenny.

"The main question is not even how the journalist got to Crimea (after all he could really be trying to make a story about how Russians are getting to Crimea), but why he made a few posts, in which he was stubbornly calling Crimea "Russian". Why did he write a report about the touristic sector in Crimea, which turned out to be very one-sided and did not cover the important questions of the annexation impact? And why is the management of that journalist unable to give an adequate response to all those questions? Anyone can make a mistake, but the task of every organization is to investigate such kind of mistakes", said Sumlenny in his comment on the Espreso website.

"The result of Rescheto's trip was a video report in English: 'Times change for the Hotels of Crimea'" — continues Homonay on Espreso.

"His video consists of two parts. In the first one Rescheto tells about a luxury hotel: an expensive one, but with a great range of services and medical care. In the second, about a hostel: it is more spartan, but also cheaper. The owner of the latter (Ukrainian by birth, but with a Russian passport, clarifies the author) says that Ukrainians almost don't visit Crimea, the say it became more expensive due to problems with logistics and increasing food prices. That is why she would be very happy to have guests

and attracts them with yoga classes, for which she purposefully conducts classes with an instructor from Moscow.

This report lacks two important nuances. First, no single word was said about how Putin packs Crimea with Russian military and Russian weapons. Second, there is no mention of such a consequence of the annexation as the Russia appropriation of the prestigious hotels, which previously belonged to the Ukrainian owners.

Particularly, on the main page of the website of the Delegation of the German Economy in Ukraine since May there is a warning that in Crimea six luxurious hotels which were previously confiscated from their rightful owners and are currently for sale. And both the German Foreign Ministry and the delegation strongly advise to not enter into agreements, since from the point of view of Ukraine and the European Union such agreements will be considered invalid.

It is clear, that Rescheto is not lying when not mentioning the arrival of more and more new Russian military equipment to Crimea and snatching of the touristic infrastructure. However, his report gives, to put in bluntly, an incomplete picture".

In the response from Deutsche Welle, which was shared on the Facebook page of the Ministry of Foreign Affairs of Ukraine, it stated: *"The journalist from Deutsche Welle, Juri Rescheto: 'I want to make a clear statement that in my journalistic work I was condemning the annexation of Crimea as the violation of the international law. Unfortunately, my interview with RT, conducted during my trip in July, was not fully reproduced therefore distorted my statements. In that interview I never made statements that Crimea is Russian, I only said that as a reporter I must reflect the reality in which people there live. And the reality is that for almost two years people have been forced to live on the Peninsula, controlled by Russia under the Russian laws. In many of my tweets you can find such hashtags, as #russia, #ukraine and #annexation. I apologize for using the hashtag #crimeaisrussian – that was a mistake. That was an omission from my side, which I deeply regret about'".*

On August 8, 2016, Ukrainian journalist Galia Koynash also posted an article about the incident on the website Kharkiv Human Rights Protection Group: „How can Deutsche Welle take part in a Russian propaganda trip to Crimea?" She made a request to Deutsche Welle and was satisfied with the response.

DW stated:

"I am asking you for an immediate correction, as you have clearly not adhered to the facts. In our coverage, DW has always maintained that the annexation of Crimea by Russia is illegitimate. There are numerous reports by the correspondents in our Kyiv bureau as well as reports from Moscow and DW editors in Germany stating this.

Our correspondent Yuri Rescheto has reported about the annexation of Crimea repeatedly, starting with reports from Crimea in the immediate follow-up to the annexation. His recent trip to Crimea was organized by the Foreign Correspondents Association in Moscow and not by the Foreign Ministry, as you claim. DW has paid for all expenses in connection with this journey.

The Kerch bridge was certainly not the main focal point, as you go on alleging. Mr. Rescheto went to Crimea on this particular occasion to report on reaction to a NATO meeting on Russia as well as to work on human rights stories.

The quotes by Mr. Rescheto in his interview with RT are taken out of context and therefore appear misleading."

Koynash's response:

"The text is about a specific visit by one journalist and his team. It is based on freely available material in either English or Russian. There were no apparent attempts to rectify the mistakes in that material which is now a month old. It is unclear what the Foreign Correspondents Association's status is, however Rescheto himself appears to state that he is in Crimea "at the invitation of the Foreign Ministry" and all reports reiterate this. It would therefore be helpful to see confirmation of this Association's organization of the trip, and its credentials for doing so. There is nothing to indicate that an attempt to agree the visit with the Ukrainian authorities was made.

The visit resulted in reports mainly for the Kremlin-funded Russia Today, and similar, about the bridge and from Artek. Searches came up with no material on the NATO meeting, nor on human rights stories, and the quotes given were clearly not out of context for the Russian media. If the Russian media reports were inaccurate, they should have been rectified. I consider that the objections I expressed to the article about tourism are legitimate, especially given that this is all that has emerged, despite the obvious need for reports on major human rights concerns.

Whether Deutsche Welle itself condemns Russia's annexation of Crimea, there is no evidence of this visit having been used for anything other than propaganda for Russia. That use was predictable and therefore preventable."

Whoever was right in this situation, Russia Today also used the participants of the trip in their propaganda.

The article which appeared on the RT website on 8 July 2016 had an unequivocally propagandist tone: *"It is now a fact: Western journalists visit Crimea, say it's now "Russian territory""*. It also said: *"Reunification with Russia has served a beneficial purpose for Crimea and its people, western reporters observed after visiting Sevastopol. They noted the "impressive" work on the 19-km bridge that will link the peninsula with the rest of Russia by 2019. Journalists from the US, the UK, Germany, South Korea, Bulgaria, Romania and Iraq have arrived in Crimea on the invitation of Russia's Foreign Ministry".*

Joining Russia was the choice of the Crimean people, Zhong Su Ha, the head of the Moscow KBS (Korean Broadcasting System) office, told RT, adding that, when he "asked the people of Crimea whether they voted for joining Russia, many people answered 'yes.' And when [he] asked them if they regret their decision they said 'no'".

The Korean journalist also said that the situation in the peninsula is now calm and comfortable adding that he "feels safe".

Many journalists also expressed their admiration for the 19km-long Crimean Bridge under construction. Once finished, this bridge, which will connect Crimea with Krasnodar region in mainland Russia, will become one of Russia's largest".

It goes without saying that the article does not mention the facts that this bridge was being constructed in violation of the law, on occupied territory, and without approval from Ukraine.

The RT article goes on:
"Corey Flintoff from Washington-based National Public Radio (NPR) has called the Crimean Bridge "an amazing piece of engineering".

"Very complex and very difficult things have been done here. So, I'm very interested in seeing, how this is done. The project takes so much time and so much energy to do something that has never been successfully done in this part of the world before," the US journalist stressed".

It also mentioned another journalist from Deutsche Welle:

"His colleague from German broadcaster Deutsche Welle, Evgeny Ush-akov, said that reports in the media didn't do justice to the scale of the work already been done in the Kerch Straight".

Other journalists were also quoted in the RT article: *"The impressions are very good. I had no idea that the construction was going at such a pace, but when the technological bridge is ready; when the piles are hammered; supports are placed – it is impressive," he said.*

> *"Following the cool down in relations between Moscow and the West over Russia's reunion with Crimea in 2014 and the conflict in Ukraine, "it's interesting for Europe to see how the people really live here; what's the infrastructure and how Russia is going to connect with Crimean Peninsula," Liviu Iurea, a correspondent for TV Romania, stressed.*

> *"With the construction underway in "such an accelerated tempo," the bridge is likely to meet its deadline, Iurea stressed.*

> *"Khalid Abdalrahman from an Iraqi broadcaster, Rudaw, said that the bridge „is a huge and interesting project for Crimea, for Russia and also for the tourists".."*

So, the RT article gave the impression that foreign journalists are supportive, that everything is calm and joyful in Crimea, and that it is being developed. All residents are cheerful and happy that they voted for integration of Crimea into the Russian federation, and that the Crimean Bridge, which was being built at that time, is a grandiose construction which leaves a deep impression.

Of course, Russia Today does not describe the repression against Crimean Tatars and other discontented people, about the colonization of the Peninsula by Russians who displaced the locals, about the seizure of attractive property, and about the fact that construction of the bridge was illegal. (After the large-scale Russian invasion of Ukraine, the bridge was used to transfer troops to occupied Crimea).

This is how disinformation about the situation on the Peninsula is spread.

Misunderstandings on this matter continued in 2022. The Ministry of Foreign Affairs of Ukraine raised claims against the Russian editorial office of Deutsche Welle for dissemination of the Russian narratives back in August 2022. The editorial office denied all accusations.

Nazism, fascism, antisemitism and other xenophobia

"Columns of thugs walk around Kyiv and other cities. They throw 'Siegs' relentlessly and shout 'Heil Zelenskiy!' It used to be 'Heil Poroshenko!' before. Nazis seek out Russian-speaking residents and attack them. Militants from the radical right-wing organization „Right Sector" did not give up on their dream of coming to Crimea to massacre the local population. Nazism, fascism, antisemitism and other xenophobia thrive in Ukraine. In the same way the Crimean Tatars did not abandon their intentions to crack down on other ethnic groups and representatives of other religions."

Such an impression can be formed if you read Crimean mass media outlets under the Russian occupation. Despite the clearly obvious facts that in Ukraine between 2016 and 2019 the position of prime minister has been held by an ethnic Jew Volodymyr Groysman. In 2019, another ethnic Jew Volodymyr Zelenskiy was elected president and continues as a wartime leader. There was a period when they were holding their positions at the same time. Were they really the ones who introduced Nazism?

There isn't a single radical nationalist party in the Ukrainian parliament. Right Sector, which was created by a volunteer battalion, is right wing. In the first years of its existence, Christians and Jews served with it as chaplains. Among its combatants were also some Muslims and one Buddhist. I have personally visited them and seen that with my own eyes. They had no religious misunderstandings. In 2014, the commander of Right Sector Dmytro Yarosh ran for president, but won fewer votes than Vadym Rabinovych, a Jewish former politician.

Only propagandists could accuse Ukrainians of Nazism.

After clearing dissenters from the information space, this is the kind of content offered by the occupiers through local media outlets. Similar accusations have been made against the locals, who stand against the occupation of Crimea by the Russians.

A Crimean human rights protection group, in collaboration with the Human Rights Center ZMINA, monitored Crimea's information space. The results were made public in 2018, in *Hate speech in the information space of Crimea* and in 2022, in *Hate speech in online media covering events in Crimea*. The first covered the period from 2014 to 2017, the second from 2018 to 2021.

The groups discovered that hate speech begins with the Russia-led Crimean officials. On the website of the government of Crimea there is a PDF version of a book by Olha Kovitidi, a „member of the Federation Council with the executive branch of the Republic of Crimea" and Maksym Grigoriev, a member of the Public Chamber of the Russian Federation and candidate of Political Science. The name of their book is *Crimea: The History of Return*. This book contains quite a few quotes from officials, which incite national enmity.

On page 63 of the book is the following statement of the "Presidium of the Supreme Council of the Autonomous Republic of Crimea", dated March 13, 2014: *"Participants of the anti-constitutional coup d'Etat have no moral right to give assessment on the legality of the all-Crimean referendum. Neo-Nazis and their supporters do not have moral right to impose their will on the inhabitants of the autonomous republic – children and grandchildren of victors over fascism. Murderers who have the blood of Crimeans and peaceful civilians on their hands – combatants of "Berkut" and Internal Troops of Ukraine do not have the moral right to set foot on the sacred Crimean land"."*

Page 339 of Kovitidi and Grigoriev's book quotes the "head" of the Crimean "parliament" Vladimir Konstantinov: *"V. Konstantinov called the situation in Crimea highly tense. He explained: people fear that "Right Sector" will come to Crimea after Maidan. Together with "Hizb-ut-Tahrir" militants and Crimean Tatar radicals they will arrange mass beatings and massacres. After all there were those, who openly threatened to slaughter the Russian population in Crimea".*

The authors of the two hate speech research papers commented: *"Such statements in the context of political repressions, which take place on the Peninsula, acquire signs of the incitement of hatred against Ukrainians, Crimean Tatars and Muslims, because since the beginning of the occupation in Crimea the accusations of membership in such organizations as "Right Sector" or "Hizb ut-Tahrir" party is used as the reason for the systematical political prosecutions of Ukrainians, Crimean Tatars and Muslims regardless of whether they belong to those organizations".*

In the materials provided by mass media in Crimea, Ukrainians are presented as "fascists", "Nazis", "Banderites". Ukraine is being called a "neofascist state" and the country's authorities a "military junta".

Numerous examples of hate speech in Crimea are authored by politicians, social activists and experts, all of whom are quoted in media outlets and directly in publications and in editorial offices.

The authors of the hate speech research come to the following conclusion: *"Due to the armed occupation of Crimea and the beginning of the military conflict on the East of Ukraine, a surge of hate speech usage has been recorded in the information space of Crimea, mostly against the residents of Ukraine.*

During this period, supporters and participants of the Euromaidan continued to become the objects of the hate speech, as a separate group of people, who stood for the European integration and participated in protests across Ukraine in winter 2013-2014. These people were mentioned by Russian propaganda in connection to various crimes more and more often. Such epithets as fascists, neo-nazis, accomplices of junta, minions of nazis, banderites, punishers and other were applied to the supporters of Euromaidan as well as to Ukrainians in general.

The speculation on the historical memory and tragedy of World War II intensified the effect and exacerbated the interethnic strife between Ukrainians and Russians, incited enmity among the participants of the military conflict at Donbass, and also aggravated the situation between inhabitants of Crimea and inhabitants of the mainland Ukraine".

Not much has changed in Crimea since 2017, but publications that were probably preparing its readers for the possible war against Ukraine began to appear.

On April 28, 2021, on the website "Politnavigator" you can find this article titled: *"Moscow has come to conclusion: Fascist Ukraine has no right for existence"*.

   "Aggression against Russia is definitely about to begin," the article says. *"We should make a clear statement: guys, if you are reviving Nazism there, excuse us, but that is already our zone of strategic interests. Here is what we have to say, and we should say the same to these bastards across the ocean. Fascist Ukraine has no right for existence. Thus, it is our existential threat, and we cannot allow the resurrection of fascism in the center of Europe, so if our partners from anti-Hitler coalition remain silent, we are not going to be silent – we will act"*.

The researchers on hate speech wrote:
"Among the analyzed content, at least 25 articles were found, where Ukrainian military were called "punishers". In addition, in other publications Ukrainian army was called "fascists", "nazis", and "descendants of Hitlerians". Thanks to the use of the World War II archetypes, these publications are targeted to incitement of the hatred against Ukraine as a state and against the Armed Forces of Ukraine"

Such publications were not included in the list of articles with demonstrations of hate speech, because they incited hatred specifically against the Armed Forces of Ukraine. However, the authors of the research believe that such publications are a powerful tool for the preparation of the separation of Ukrainian society, based on the principle of „friend or foe". As residents of Ukraine, who live in the occupied territories of Crimea and Donbass, and who are being called "Russians" and victims of the "Ukrainian punishers", prove those authors' attempts to separate the residents of Ukraine, based on their ethnicity.

   These publications not only urge the destruction of Ukrainian soldiers, but also threaten their family members. For example, such a deterrence is present on a website "Novorosinform", dated May 17, 2021, under the title *Burn in hell*: *"Youth of LPR posted a farewell video for the 14th brigade of the Armed Forces of Ukraine"*, which included a video clip.

The researchers found:

"In addition to military, whom they called punishers, nazis, murderers, the video discloses personal data (first and last names and photos of families of servicemen), shows light and peaceful photos of Ukrainian families in contrast with photos of ruined houses and videos of civil objects destruction. The video was shot against the background of ruins and a teddy bear.

So, the negativity extends to servicemen families, who live happily (according to the photos), while their husbands and fathers kill children in Donbass. In this video the civilians — families of servicemen — become the objects of hatred. Making their full names and photos public may threaten safety.

Such kind of content contributes to the destruction of the Ukrainian identity among the residents of the frontline and occupied territories. The hatred against the Ukrainian army and the state of Ukraine resulting from these publications becomes a strong springboard for further incitement of hatred against all Ukrainians based on ethnicity".

This brief overview after February 24, 2022, when more extensive aggression against Ukraine began, gives a clear understanding of the systematic incitement of hatred against Ukraine and Ukrainians on the Crimean Peninsula. Drop by drop the Russian mass media were preparing public opinion for war.

I have put a full stop, having read the text and got the impression of a solid hopelessness. This journalist was beaten, that one was convicted, someone else was taken to the basement and hit there, and the other one's equipment was seized. The occupation authorities are doing everything they want, and there seems to be nothing to oppose it.

In fact, the Russian government resorts to arbitrary mayhem, but the resistance to this mayhem is considerable. The prosecutor's office of the ARC working on the mainland territory of Ukraine studies the information from various sources carefully, opens dozens of criminal proceedings on violations of the rights of journalists in the occupied peninsula and investigates into the same. A large number of NGOs, such as the Crimean Human Rights Group, Human Rights Information Center, Krym-SOS, Ukrainian Helsinki Human Rights Union and others have been monitoring the situation in Crimea continuously, transferring the data to the law enforcement agencies and conveying this information to the global community. The Crimean journalists and whole editor's offices forced to leave Crimea continue to operate in mainland Ukraine, obtain and disseminate information despite everything, avoiding various obstacles and blockades.

At a first glance, this work is devoid of sense. It is impossible to overcome Russia in its territory. The justice system is completely subordinate to the government there, and renders politically motivated judgments. However, the situation in the world is changing very quickly; it will change in Russia, too, under the pressure of various circumstances, and then the collected materials will serve as a good basis to bring criminals to justice.

Largely due to this work, the world does not forget that Crimea remains Ukrainian and does not agree to the blind eye of the illegal annexation. During the international events of various levels, the representatives of the international community repeat that the peninsula belongs to Ukraine, and insist on its return.

Western countries use other means of influence, including economic sanctions against the aggressor. Moscow might pretend indifference, but they work every day, eroding the foundation of the existing regime. The time will come, and it will fall down like a house of cards.

This book, too, was written in order to precipitate this moment of the future. Recent events fill me with special hope. The armed forces of Ukraine will liberate the occupied territories step-by-step. Perhaps, when this book will be published, the Ukrainian flag will be flying over Crimea again. Or the situation will be close to that. I can say with confidence that the heroes of my book also made their contribution to our victory. After all, the information space in this war is no less important than the one where guns are fired. Ukrainian journalists, about whom I have the honor to write, turned out to be real fighters.

1. *Chongar* is the checkpoint on the administrative border between Crimea and mainland Russia (page 1)

Friends of the Series

The book makes an important contribution to documenting the start of the annexation and another proof that in any war, the media are the first to be attacked.
It provides a small insight into a very important mission that my team and I conducted in Crimea on the eve of the illegal annexation.
It was essential for me to be able to talk directly with the journalists facing repression and under attack so I could give my frank and direct assessment to all 57 OSCE States that there is ongoing information war in Ukraine.

Dunja Mijatovic,
OSCE Representative
on Freedom of the Media (2010 - 2017)

The suppression of media freedom in Russia has been a central enabling strategy for Russia's current full-scale invasion of Ukraine.
Silencing of independent and critical journalism provided the regime with an unprecedented control over the public discourse and extinguished dissenting voices.
This book documents how in 2014, when Russia occupied and illegally annexed Crimea, the suppression of journalism was one of their first and immediate priorities. It is a text-book case study of oppression written often as if in real time. Journalism as eyewitness to history.

Frane Maroevich,
International Press Institute,
Executive Director.

In this book, along with the consistent coverage of the tragic eventsof 2014 and the following years, related to the persecution of freemass media and independent journalists in the Russian-occupied Crimea,society also received important documentary evidence about the crimescommitted by the Russian occupation authorities in Crimea.
Since the author of the book himself was in Crimea during the dayswhen

the peninsula was captured by Russian troops, his personalobservations immerse the reader in a disturbing atmosphere when acarelessly spoken word could cost a journalist life or freedom.

Rephat Chubarov,
Head of Crimean Tatar People Majlis.

ibidem.eu